MORE KITCHEN WISDOM

ALSO BY FRIEDA ARKIN
Kitchen Wisdom

MORE
Kitchen Wisdom

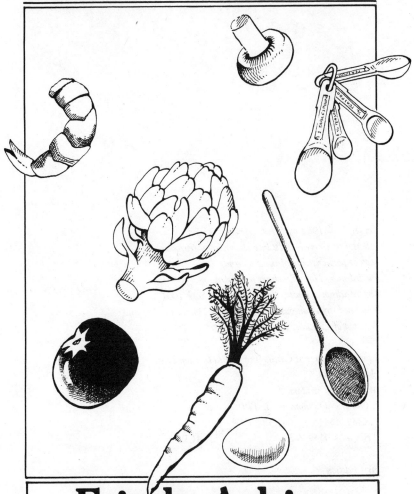

Frieda Arkin

HOLT, RINEHART AND WINSTON NEW YORK

Copyright © 1982 by Frieda Arkin
All rights reserved, including the right to reproduce this
book or portions thereof in any form.
Published by Holt, Rinehart and Winston,
383 Madison Avenue, New York, New York 10017.
Published simultaneously in Canada by Holt, Rinehart and
Winston of Canada, Limited.

Library of Congress Cataloging in Publication Data
Arkin, Frieda.
More kitchen wisdom.
1. Cookery–Dictionaries. I. Title.
TX349.A683   641.5′03′21   81-7188
ISBN 0-03-055376-8   AACR2

First Edition

Designer: Joy Chu
Illustrations by Kate Lanxner

Printed in the United States of America
10 9 8 7 6 5 4 3 2 1

ISBN 0-03-055376-8

INTRODUCTION

I have to confess that at one time in my life I regarded the kitchen as a battlefield. There were all those stolid appliances daring me to put a hand to them. And there were the foods whose days or hours were numbered. Not only might they perish, but they were often delicate and imbued with what seemed to be a built-in propensity for misbehaving—for "not coming out right."

I wasn't alone in these convictions, either. I discovered that many of my friends admitted to a certain timidity when entering the kitchen. We never knew for sure whether the meal we had in mind would end up even remotely resembling our mental picture of it—to say nothing of the intimidating photographs in the recipe book. (And—rarity of rarities—when the meal *did* succeed, how we crowed. It seemed a miracle.)

Perhaps this timidity in the kitchen is one reason that packaged foods of all kinds are so popular: premixed cakes, cookies, pies, puddings, and other desserts; instant soups, instant mashed potatoes, instant this, instant that; and on and on. Frozen meals, too, of course. Preparing dishes from these premixed, instant, and frozen foods is not just a matter of saving time. It's also buying the myth that packaged foods are practically *guaranteed* not to fail—though the nutrition, flavor, quality, and price might leave something to be desired.

One way to alleviate kitchen-fright and overcome dependency on packaged foods is simply to learn how to gain the upper hand in the kitchen and come out victorious. It's not so hard, even for someone with mildly epicurean tastes. True, it takes a little courage and a little time, but you *can* learn the nature of foods and how they behave. In quick order, you can acquire a fund of "how-tos" to put to immediate use. It often happens, once you open your perceptions to this sort of empirical learning, that solutions to problems seem to leap out of the air. They did for me. As I began to wield sieves and whisks and knives and spoons, new ideas and discoveries suddenly bloomed in my mind. "Here's how to do it!" I'd exult, when I ran a particular problem to the ground and it became a problem no longer.

Of course I also welcomed many ideas, discoveries, and suggestions passed on to me by others, all of which I tested.

That's how *Kitchen Wisdom* was born.

As I continued my work in the kitchen, with an eye to further problem-solving and to the successful serving of fine meals, I amassed more and more bits of wisdom to add to what I had before.

That's how *More Kitchen Wisdom* came into being.

Most cooks acquire their kitchen learning by reading and watching and listening and doing. In the process, they learn that there is often more than one way to do things in the kitchen. For cooks who welcome new and different procedures, this book may make time spent in the kitchen more fruitful and more enjoyable.

I wish you all the same pleasure in putting these ideas to use as I had in collecting them and working them out. You will learn, as I have, that no matter how much we know about cooking and food there is always room for more kitchen wisdom.

Have you any culinary discoveries you'd like to share? Any wise suggestions or bright solutions to kitchen problems?

If so, Frieda Arkin and her publisher, Holt, Rinehart and Winston, would appreciate knowing about them. Write:

Box 34
Essex, Massachusetts 01929.

MORE KITCHEN WISDOM

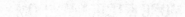

ALMONDS: see NUTS

APPETIZERS: see HORS D'OEUVRES

APPLES

■ the tastiest red and yellow eating apples are those that show a little green at both the flower end and the stem end.

■ it's very hard to find eating apples nowadays that haven't, alas, had some wax applied to them. Your best bet is to peel before eating. Apples for cooking and baking, however, are rarely waxed.

■ if you want baked apples that won't develop wrinkled skins, make a few short slits here and there in the apples before you set them in the oven, or use a potato peeler to pare a narrow band around the center of the apples.

■ for a treat, pour a little port wine over baked apples just before you take them from the oven.

■ when you're making large quantities of peeled, cut apples, toss them in a mixture of 1 cup of cold water and 1 tablespoon of vinegar or lemon juice. Keeping the apples in this mixture until you're ready to use them will prevent them from discoloring.

APPLESAUCE

■ if you like your applesauce to have a rosy pink color,

wash and core red apples and cook them whole with their skins on. Purée them afterward, skins and all.

- to make applesauce without cooking, simply drop pieces of peeled apple in the blender and add a little lemon juice. You can also add some sugar or honey if you like, or a touch of nutmeg or cinnamon.

APRICOTS
- apricots spoil rapidly once they're bruised. Be sure you handle them carefully when packing or unpacking them. Because they don't keep well–they quickly become mealy and tasteless–eat them within a couple of days of buying.

APRONS
- the best apron is one that covers you to the neck. Also, big pockets are useful for that towel you're always wiping your hands on.

ARTICHOKES
- pick artichokes by weight, not size; the heavier, the better. And be sure the leaves are green and tightly closed.
- don't buy artichokes if the leaves are open; they're overmature, have little flavor, and are inclined to be woody.
- it's traditional to dip cooked artichoke leaves in melted butter, but you can use dozens of other dips: mayonnaise or sour cream mixtures, or other sauces you dream up.
- try dicing cooked or canned artichoke hearts or artichoke bottoms into very small bits and adding them to an omelet.

ASPARAGUS
- 1 pound of asparagus will usually serve 3 people.
- fresh asparagus have tightly closed tips. If the tips have

begun to spread, the asparagus aren't fresh and have lost a lot of flavor.

■ fresh young asparagus are delicious raw. Wash, and serve with a mayonnaise sauce. Or cut them up to use in salads.

■ you can use a percolator coffeepot to cook asparagus vertically. Asparagus, like spaghetti, should be cooked *al dente*.

AVOCADO

■ one medium-sized avocado, cubed, will give you about 1½ cups.

■ light-brown markings on the skin of an avocado don't mean anything in particular, but if the spots are dark and sunken, this is usually a sign of decay inside.

■ avocados don't ripen well in the refrigerator. If you have one that is too hard and green to use right away, keep it in a dark warm place for a few days. Check it daily, though.

■ if you're buying an avocado for mashing, buy it a little riper than you ordinarily might. It should be very soft and its skin uniformly dark, not just dark in spots.

■ if you're making an avocado dip, such as guacamole, be sure to include lemon juice in the mixture so the avocado will keep its green-yellow color and not darken.

BACON

- here's a way to have bacon cooked and ready when you want it. Fry the slices ahead of time, drain them, then wrap in waxed paper. Freeze in a plastic bag or other freezer container. When you want to use them—they thaw quickly—just place in a skillet and heat.

- a small amount of bacon fat is a tasty addition to corn bread or corn muffin batter.

BAGELS

- an easy way to shape bagels from dough is to make a ball of dough just as you would when you make rolls. Then dip your index finger in flour and poke it through the middle of the ball. Whirl the dough around your finger until the opening is the size you want.

BAKING

- see also *Energy Savers, Ovens.*

- save on fuel! Plan your meals so that when you're baking or roasting a main dish, you're also baking or roasting something else: a baked vegetable dish to be served with what you're roasting, or a cake or a pudding for dessert, or a dish to be served in the future which you can freeze.

- in a top-of-stove baker you can bake a couple of potatoes or cook individual servings of frozen foods without having to heat a large oven. These economical bakers are made to fit over a burner, but be sure to get one with a snugly fitting top.

■ for proper circulation of heat in the oven, place cake or pie pans so they don't touch one another or the oven walls.

■ if you have to keep an oven-cooked dish warm but don't want it to become soggy, leave it in the oven and cover it with aluminum foil pierced in the middle to let out the steam.

BAKING POWDER

■ baking powder keeps its potency for about a year and a half. Because it deteriorates with age, to test to see if it's still active, add ¼ teaspoon of baking powder to 1 tablespoon of water. If the baking powder bubbles, it's fresh enough to use.

BAKING SODA

■ baking soda is affected by moisture in the air. Once you open a box, pour the contents into a jar with a tight screw cap. It will keep longer.

■ like baking powder, baking soda's potency deteriorates with age. To test for freshness, add ¼ teaspoon of baking soda to 1 tablespoon of vinegar. If the baking soda bubbles, it's usable.

BANANAS

■ one ripe medium-sized banana will give you ½ cup sliced and ⅓ cup mashed.

■ buy bananas on the green side and let them ripen at home. They're one of the few fruits that improve after they've been picked green. The very yellow bananas in the stores have often been artificially ripened by gas. They don't taste as good as those that ripen naturally and slowly in your own kitchen.

■ lemon juice will keep peeled bananas from darkening.

STORING AND FREEZING

■ bananas *can* be stored in the refrigerator. The skins will darken, but the bananas themselves will stay firmer and fresher than if you keep them at room temperature.

■ bananas can be frozen. Don't peel them. Pop them in the freezer until you want them. Then hold them under warm water for about 1 minute. They defrost quite quickly, but are best used when sliced into a fruit salad while they're still a little frozen.

■ another way of freezing bananas is to mash them, add a little lemon juice to keep them white, and put in a covered container in the freezer (leave room for expansion). You can use them in baking any time you like.

■ you can also slice bananas, lay the slices out on a cookie sheet, and freeze. Store the frozen slices in a plastic bag. Use in banana pie, fruit salads, and for snacks.

DESSERTS AND OTHER DELICACIES

■ fully ripe bananas–preferably those with brown spots on them–are the best to use for banana bread, milk shakes, etc. Such bananas are not only softer, but they also have more flavor.

■ you can put whole bananas, with their skins on, right on the grill the next time you have a cookout. Cook about 8 minutes, turning several times. They're wonderful.

■ to bake bananas, peel them, put them in a baking dish, brush with lime juice, and pour a little white wine mixed with honey over them. Dot with butter or margarine and bake at 400° F for 30 minutes, until they're lightly browned. Baste them now and then. What a dessert!

■ to make a banana layer cake, add an extra egg to regular white cake batter and 1½ cups of very ripe mashed banana. Also add ½ teaspoon of baking soda to the dry ingredients.

- to make a lovely cake icing out of mashed bananas, add a little soft butter, lemon juice, cream, and some confectioners' sugar. Mix well.
- you can also mash bananas into pancake batter to make banana fritters.
- here's a low calorie substitute for whipped cream that's thick and delicious: Whip an egg white until it's stiff, then whip in a ripe banana, one thick slice at a time. You don't even need to add sugar. A touch of vanilla extract, maybe, or some honey.
- if you leave a banana in the freezer until it's semifrozen, it will have the consistency of sherbet. Peel it, put it in a dish, and, if your taste so inclines, dribble a little chocolate syrup over it when you serve it.

BARBECUING

- charcoal absorbs moisture readily. Store it in airtight plastic bags. It will ignite faster.
- if rain forces you indoors, remember that most recipes for barbecuing chicken or meat on an outdoor spit are easily adapted to oven roasting. Cook in a low oven and baste often.

BASIL: see HERBS AND SPICES

BASTING

- pieces of suet or unrendered fat placed over a roasting bird or piece of meat automatically baste the bird or meat.
- if you have the leafy ends of some celery stalks handy when you need to baste meat, chicken, or fish, use this "nature's brush" for your basting. You can then cut up the leaves and use them in gravy. A small bunch of parsley can be used for this, too. You won't have to wash a basting brush.

BATTER

- see also *Blender, Cake, Pancakes.*
- batter containing flour will get thicker on standing. So if you mix a batter and don't use it right away, add a tiny bit of milk or water just before you're ready to use it, then beat it a little.

BEAN SPROUTS

- if you're sprouting mung or other types of beans in a jar, remember that the sprouts increase to about five times the volume of the original beans. Be sure you choose a jar that will allow room for this.

BEANS

- like rice, dried beans and lentils expand greatly during cooking. A cup of raw beans or lentils will increase to 2 or 2½ cups after cooking.
- when you buy a package of dried beans, be sure they are of uniform size. Small beans cook faster than large ones.
- also pick beans that are bright and uniform in color. If they show fading, they've been stored too long.
- you can get rid of the gassiness produced by cooked dried beans if you soak them for 2 or 3 hours before cooking. Throw away the soaking water, cover with boiling water and cook for half an hour. Discard that water too. Cover with more boiling water and cook until the beans are done. The result is very tender and nongassy beans.
- dried beans should be cooked slowly. Too high heat breaks them up and makes them stick to the pot.

BEEF: see MEATS

BEEF HEART: see PRESSURE COOKER

BEETS
- 2 pounds of fresh beets will serve 4 to 6 people.
- beet greens are really delightful in salad, especially young tender ones. If you're going to cook beets to serve as a vegetable course, cut off the greens and wash and chill them. Then shred them and mix with lettuce or other salad vegetables, to serve separately or the next day. Tough greens can be cooked and served much like spinach.
- baked beets are twice as good as boiled ones. Scrub but don't peel them. Bake at 325° F for at least an hour or until the beets have totally shrunk away from the skin and the skin itself is thoroughly wrinkled. The flavor of baked beets is truly marvelous.

BERRIES
- you will need 4 cups of fresh berries to make a 9-inch pie.
- don't wash berries until you need them. Wet berries don't keep as long in the refrigerator as dry ones. But if you have washed berries and must store them, spread them on a towel to dry before you put them in the refrigerator.
- for an unusual dessert, freeze washed and drained berries in a flat serving dish, then at serving time remove from the freezer and pour cream over them. The cream will freeze slightly to the berries. The combination is wonderful.
- fresh berries that are frozen and then thawed release much of their juices. If you're going to make fruit sauce or jelly or jam, freeze the berries first; the result will be much richer.
- if you're making a pie or pudding using frozen berries instead of fresh ones, use less liquid and a little more thickener because frozen berries are much juicier when thawed than fresh ones.
- a great way to freeze berries for storage is to lay them

out flat in plastic bags (you can sprinkle a little sugar over them if you like) and set the bags in the freezer. When you want to defrost some, break off a piece of the frozen sheet of berries. There's no need to defrost the whole package.

■ when you're serving berries as a dessert, try pouring wine over them instead of cream.

■ if you're making a blueberry pie with fresh berries, bake the crust first; then cook the berry filling on top of the stove, using only half the berries. When the filling is cooked, combine gently with the rest of the uncooked berries. Fill the baked pie crust and chill. You'll get the nicest blueberry pie ever.

■ 1 pound of cranberries equals about 4 cups; it will also give you 4 cups of cranberry sauce.

■ cranberries should be cooked only until they "pop"– about 5 minutes.

■ to give not-so-sweet strawberries a richer flavor, wash them quickly in cool water, pat dry with a towel, remove the hulls, then stand the berries, hulled side down, on a tray that has been sprinkled with white granulated or light-brown sugar. Cover lightly with paper towels and let stand at room temperature for a few hours.

■ when you prepare strawberries for a pie, always wash and pat them dry with a towel before removing the hulls. Then set them to drain on layers of paper toweling. This will get rid of the excess moisture and your pie won't be mushy.

BISCUITS

■ to make your baking powder biscuits split open neatly for buttering, roll out the dough about ¼ inch thick, fold half of this over onto the other half, and cut into biscuits.

■ you can form biscuits quickly if you roll out the biscuit dough into a rectangle and use a knife dipped in flour to cut into squares for baking. (Who says biscuits have to be round?)

■ baking powder biscuits get slightly smaller when they're baked, so you can set them rather close together on the baking sheet.

■ to reheat biscuits with very little trouble, cover a very heavy pot or a large skillet tightly and heat for 5 minutes over medium heat. Turn off the heat, put the biscuits in, cover again, and let stand for about 10 minutes.

BLENDER

■ the blender is a very handy piece of kitchen equipment and it isn't very expensive. It's remarkable for the things it can do: puréeing, making smooth gravies and sauces, making foamy drinks, and much more.

■ you can make practically every kind of salad dressing in the blender. It's quick, nonmessy, and the emulsion (the even mixing of the oil and the vinegar or lemon juice) seems to hold longer. If you want to add small chunks of solids such as blue cheese to the dressing, add them after the dressing has been blendered.

■ the mayonnaise you make in a blender is more delicate and delicious, and much less expensive, than store-bought mayonnaise. Most cookbooks contain at least one mayonnaise recipe you can make in a blender.

■ when you make a cake, try blendering the granulated sugar slightly before adding it to the batter. This gives the cake a more delicate texture and the crumb will be more finely grained.

■ a blender is great for taking the lumps out of brown sugar.

■ if you're out of confectioners' sugar, you can make a nearly perfect substitute by putting granulated sugar in the blender and grinding it until it becomes powdery. But be careful not to overdo it—the sugar may begin to caramelize.

- use the blender to fine-grind small amounts of nuts.

- for grated orange or lemon peel, first peel the orange or lemon into thin strips with a potato peeler. Then drop the strips into the blender. Presto: grated peel.

- you can make delicious hot soups by using up many cooked leftovers. Combine them with some stock or other liquid and necessary seasonings. Into the blender, and you have a great soup! Add sour cream (or yogurt) to the leftovers and stock in the blender, and you've got a great cold soup.

- if you want to thicken a vegetable soup, pour a cup or more of the soup–including some of the vegetables or other solids–into the blender. Mix until it's well puréed. Once this is poured back into the soup, the soup will be tastily thickened without the addition of a single calorie.

- use the blender to grind up leftovers to make unusual sauces or gravies to go over vegetables, meat, fish, or chicken.

- no need to grate the skin off your fingers every time you need some grated cheese. Dice the cheese into small pieces and drop these into the blender (if the pieces are too large they may get stuck in the blades). The drier the cheese, the finer it can be grated.

- the blender does a nice job of grinding nutmeg and cloves. Set your blender at high speed and drop in half a nutmeg, then clamp on the lid. When you want ground cloves, you can drop in several at a time. The flavor is much better than that of ready-ground spices. You will probably end up with more than you need, so bottle it. It will always be fresher than store-bought.

- try substituting a different kind of flour for an equal amount of white flour in any bread, roll, or cookie recipe. With the blender, ½ cup or more of uncooked Wheatena, for example, can be ground up quite fine, and it adds a marvelous nutty quality to a home-baked bread. Similarly, you can use almost any uncooked or dry cereal—oats, bran, any rice cereal, corn flakes, etc. For bread doughs, there are infinite variations. You can substitute for an equal amount of white flour uncooked split peas ground up in the blender—what an aromatic flour that makes! You can also use any kind of dried beans, lentils, or barley.

■ you can grind coffee in the blender—though not all blenders are well suited to the task. Buy whole coffee beans and grind each day's supply as you need it. And you can make it as fine as you like, depending on the kind of coffee maker you use. (Actually, the finer the grind, the fuller the flavor.)

■ when you make bran or corn muffins, mix the wet ingredients for the batter in the blender. Pour this into the flour mixture and mix quickly by hand. There's less chance of overmixing the batter this way.

■ you can also use the blender to mix pancake batter— everything goes in for about 15 seconds.

■ overcooked steak or a leftover piece of roast are the fixings for a first-rate pâté. Cut the meat into small chunks and feed the pieces into the blender with some Worcestershire sauce, a little mayonnaise, any spices you like, a bit of salt and pepper. Cover little bread squares or crackers with this to serve as canapés with drinks, or as appetizers, or with soup. Or use as a sandwich spread.

■ put leftover cooked fish into the blender and make it into a pâté, just as you would meat or chicken. Add mayonnaise or other moisteners, herbs, and other flavors. This is especially good for a celery or egg stuffing, or for a canapé spread.

■ when making a white sauce, pour all the ingredients, including the butter, into the blender and set it going. When it's thoroughly mixed, pour into a wet rinsed-out pan and heat, stirring with a whisk, until it's thickened. You won't have to worry about lumps and it's easier than melting the butter, adding flour, mixing, adding warmed liquid, etc. Try it.

■ make your own bread crumbs by breaking up slices of stale bread, including the crusts, and dropping the pieces into the blender with salt, pepper, powdered garlic, and dry cheese or any herbs you have on hand. (Cut the cheese into small pieces first.) In this way you get more variety than with store-bought bread crumbs—and for less cost.

■ aerate fruit drinks in the blender. Orange juice made from frozen concentrate is twice as tasty if you blender it before serving. You can fizz up tomato juice in the same way.

■ vegetables, fruits, meats, or chicken can be puréed in the blender, then frozen in small quantities (in ice cube trays, for instance) to be used as baby food.

■ many a blender will clean itself. After you've used it, put in some water and a tiny bit of soap or detergent and turn it on. Run until the blades are clean. Rinse well.

■ if the blade attachment of your blender can be removed, put the attachment in a container and cover it with cooking oil. Do this every few months, letting it stand overnight. Then drain, wash, and rinse. This will allow the blade mechanism to turn freely and with less resistance when the blender is on.

BLUEBERRIES: see BERRIES

BOTTLES: see JARS AND BOTTLES

BRASS: see COPPER

BREAD
■ see also *Blender, Bread Crumbs, Yeast and Yeast Dough.*

DOUGH

If the prospect of wrestling with a big lump of dough discourages you from bread making, you might try this. Most bread recipes are for 2 loaves, but you can halve the recipe and make a single loaf. Not only is it much easier to work with a small ball of dough, but also the smaller the volume of dough, the faster it rises. The entire bread-making session will take less time. And for many people, a single loaf of bread is enough.

- for half the amount of white flour in your bread dough, substitute barley or dried beans or lentils, or any dry cereal such as oats or Wheatena that has been finely ground in the blender. Mix well in the blender with the white flour. Your bread will be very tasty indeed.

- add a teaspoon of garlic powder to your flour when making bread. You'll have a lightly garlic-flavored bread that is delicious, especially warmed or toasted.

- if you want to add more gluten to your bread flour but still don't want the dough to be coarse, substitute ½ cup or so of sifted whole wheat flour for the same amount of white flour. If you have siftings left over in the sieve (and this depends on the size of the openings in the sieve), use these siftings—called bran siftings—in other breads or add to your bread crumb supply.

- sugarless varieties of crisp dry cereal add a fine touch to bread dough. Substitute ½ cup or so, just as it comes from the package, for ½ cup of flour.

- some bread bakers feel that the chlorine in our water supply systems inhibits the growth of yeasts. This may be true, but there's no need to buy spring water for making bread. Chlorine is volatile, so it will disappear if you boil the water for a few minutes, especially in the small quantities used for bread dough. (Be sure to cool the water to body temperature before you add yeast, however, or you'll kill the yeast.)

■ if you want to make a crusty bread with a wheaty flavor, use water as your liquid. If you like a soft crust with a creamy white crumb, use whole or skimmed milk.

■ bread made with milk has a softer, more tender crust than bread made with water. This is one reason that bakers often prefer to use milk if the dough is intended for rolls.

■ don't imagine that you have to limit yourself to water or milk for the liquid when making bread. Although most recipes call for one of these liquids, you can substitute others. A rich strong broth is marvelous in a bread dough, so if you have some soup around, strain it and use a cup or so—whatever volume of liquid the recipe calls for—in your bread. Or don't even strain it; put it in the blender and use the purée. You'll need a little less flour if you do this.

■ you can also use vegetable juices of any kind (including the water you cook vegetables in) when making bread. And if the bread is a sweet one, use fruit juice.

■ when making a fruit bread with baking powder dough, let the mixed dough stand in the baking pan for 20 minutes before you put it in the oven. This seems to mellow and ripen the bread, giving it a richer flavor.

■ if you find handling yeast dough difficult, oil your hands with cooking oil first.

■ it's probably impossible to knead bread dough too much, so go to town on it. Knead for at least 10 minutes. Knock it around, turn it over now and then, smack it down hard on the kneading surface. It thrives on rough treatment.

■ you can often mix and knead bread dough in the same bowl. Use one of those huge 17- or 18-inch stainless steel bowls for mixing and kneading. This has another advantage: You can move the bowl to a higher or lower surface, thus varying the height at which you work to ease the strain on your back and shoulder muscles.

■ you'll have no trouble getting bread dough to rise easily if you put it in a warm oven. For either a gas or electric oven, bring the temperature to warm (but not so warm that you can't rest your hand comfortably on the baking rack). Turn off the heat and put in the bowl of dough to rise. Check after 30 minutes—you may need to warm the oven slightly again. (Remove the bowl before rewarming the oven.)

■ if you use plastic wrap to cover a bowl or pan of bread dough while it's rising, oil the underside of the plastic first, otherwise the dough will stick to it. If you've forgotten to do this and the dough does stick, dip the blade of a table knife in oil and use this for removing the dough from the plastic.

■ you'll get a lighter loaf of bread if you knead the dough again a short time after the dough has completed its first rising. Allow the dough to rise once more before you put it in the pan for the second and final rising before baking.

■ if you're making a rye or whole wheat bread, the height to which the loaf will ultimately rise depends somewhat on the ratio of the white flour to the heavier flour—the more white, the more volume.

■ if you're making a single loaf of bread, you need not grease a separate bowl for the dough to rise in. Instead, oil the baking pan and let the dough do its first rising in this. When it has risen, take it out of the pan, knead it a little, sprinkle the oiled pan with a little flour, and replace the dough for the second and final rising. When it's risen and ready to bake, put the pan in the preheated oven. (Actually, you can do this if you're baking 2 loaves. Divide the original dough into halves after you've kneaded it and let each half rise in its own baking pan, as above.)

■ when making bread in a cold kitchen, warm all the ingredients, including the flour and the mixing bowl in a low oven before mixing. Your dough will rise higher.

▪ a batter bread is one that requires no kneading. The unbaked dough has a higher proportion of liquid to flour, but you pour it into the baking pan much as you would a cake batter. The baked loaf is more moist than a kneaded bread and also somewhat coarser.

▪ you'll get a nice moist loaf of bread if you add a ½ cup of well-cooked, blendered rice to your bread.

▪ a little mashed potato added to bread dough will give the bread a most attractive flavor.

▪ use little or no shortening when you make the dough if you want a bread that's dry and crispy like some Italian or French breads. Remember, this type of bread dries out much faster than regular bread.

BAKING

▪ if you want to serve freshly baked bread or rolls at your dinner party but don't have time to make them on the day of your dinner, make them days ahead and *partially* bake them. Then wrap them individually in aluminum foil or waxed paper and freeze. Thaw them on the morning of the day of your dinner. Just before they are to be served, put them in the oven and finish baking. They'll taste exactly as though you'd started from scratch the same day.

▪ if you have to make bread on a day when you know you're going to be rushed, measure out all the ingredients the night before, refrigerating those which need it. Then in the morning you can just go to it. This is a great time saver.

▪ here's an unusual bread for you: When the dough is ready for the final rising, press in only half the amount of dough, and then spoon a thin layer of cooked, seasoned ground meat on top of this. Put the remainder of the dough on top of the meat layer, press down gently, and let the whole thing rise.

Then bake as usual. What a wonderful bread!

■ if you want to bake a round loaf of bread, bake it in a casserole dish, 1½- to 2-quart size.

■ to prevent the crust of a bread from cracking, make shallow, diagonal slashes across the top of the unbaked loaf just before you set it in the oven to bake.

■ to get a very crunchy crust on breads and rolls, baste them with ice water after they've been baking for 10 minutes. You can also put a pan of water in the oven with the baking bread. It's the humidity that gives the "crunch."

■ if you want to have an interesting speckled crust on the top of bread or rolls—the kind of crust on Dutch bread—brush the surface with beaten egg white at 20-minute intervals or so during the final rising.

■ freshly baked bread is difficult to cut; but if you must cut, heat the knife blade first.

■ for professional-looking crusts for breads or rolls, brush the tops with milk and dust with flour before baking.

■ if the bread you're baking seems to be developing a hard crust too soon, cover the entire bread with a large heat-proof bowl or a pot, and continue baking. Remove the covering about 10 minutes before the bread has finished baking.

■ Italian-style breadsticks can be made from any bread dough. After the dough has risen, pull off pieces about the size of walnuts and roll them into pencil-thin ropes. Put them on lightly greased cookie sheets, pressing the ends down firmly. Brush with milk or beaten egg yolk and sprinkle with caraway, poppy, or sesame seeds (and salt if you like). Bake in a hot oven till crisp.

■ bread containing whole eggs tends to brown quickly. If you see this happening, cover it lightly with aluminum foil halfway through the baking period.

■ if your bread doesn't seem completely baked when you remove it from the pan, let the bread continue baking, out of the pan, on the oven rack.

■ bread baked in a heavy metal pan will not readily brown on the sides and bottom.

■ no two ovens bake alike. Every bread baker has to adapt the bread recipe, temperature, and baking time to the oven. Don't be afraid to make changes and substitutions if your bread doesn't turn out the way you want it the first time. Just keep track of which substitutions help to produce the desired results.

STORING

■ never wrap a newly baked loaf of bread until it's thoroughly cooled; otherwise it will sweat and become soggy.

■ unless you freeze bread, keep it at room temperature in a container that allows a little air to get in. Bread kept in plastic bags loses its crispness.

■ remember that whole wheat and other dark breads are almost impossible to slice when they're thoroughly frozen. Slice the breads before you freeze them. And if you slip small pieces of waxed paper between the slices, they will be easier to separate.

■ some cooks tend to think that freshly baked bread is going to spoil quickly. Actually, it will keep for about a week at normal room temperature without developing mold. But in very warm weather, slice the bread, wrap it well, and pop it in the freezer.

ODDS AND ENDS

■ to butter very thin slices of bread (when making hors

d'oeuvres, for instance), start with an unsliced loaf. Slice off the end of the loaf (you can use it for croutons) and spread softened butter on the cut end of the loaf. Slice as thin as you wish, butter the next cut end, and repeat to the end of the loaf.

■ if you have a few slices of bread that you won't be eating, set them in a very low oven (200° F or less) until they're crisp and tanned. This is Melba toast, and it will keep for weeks.

■ dice bread crusts and sauté them in oil or butter with any spices or flavorings you like. They make wonderful croutons for soup or salad. And if you don't want to make croutons immediately, freeze the diced crusts until you're ready.

■ the sandwich syndrome makes us think bread has to be cut into slices. If it's Italian or French bread, tear it into chunks to eat. You get more of the substance, taste, and aroma this way. And if you've just baked a bread, cut it into large cubes instead of slices to get the really homemade flavor.

BREAD CRUMBS
■ see also *Blender, Breading.*
■ 3 slices of fresh white bread, finely chopped or crumbled, will give you 1¾ cups of soft crumbs; 3 slices of welldried white bread will give you ½ cup of dry crumbs.

■ if you have extra slices of bread, dry them, grate them, and add to your bread crumb supply.

■ to make bread crumbs, dry out slices of bread by putting them into a wire lettuce basket or a string shopping bag, and hang in your kitchen until the slices become crisp. Exposing them on all sides this way will give you uniform drying.

■ you can also dry slices of bread in a very low oven until they're thoroughly crisp.

■ if you don't have a blender, put thoroughly dried slices

of bread in a clear plastic bag, press the air out, and close the open end. Crush with a rolling pin until the crumbs are very fine.

■ you can grate bread crumbs as you need them by storing a well-wrapped roll or two in the freezer. Grate the frozen roll over the surface of the dish you want the bread crumbs on, much as you would grate a piece of cheese.

■ if you're out of bread crumbs and don't even have any stale bread around, use dry cereals. Any of them can be tossed into the blender, and spiced and flavored in any way you like. If you don't have a blender, cover them with a dish towel and run a rolling pin over them.

BREADING

■ corn flakes ground into fine crumbs give a nice crunchy coating for chicken or fish.

■ you can make a breading (of crumbs, flour, etc.) adhere very nicely to fish fillets, chops, or chicken pieces if you first cover the pieces of food with a mixture of 2 parts skimmed milk powder and 1 part water. Let the pieces stand in this coating for 5 minutes, then shake well before dipping them in the breading. Fry or sauté.

■ a bread crumb crust will adhere better to chicken, fish, chops, etc., if you put the breaded food in the refrigerator for an hour or so before frying or sautéing.

BROILING

■ broiling is a cinch as long as you don't place the food too close to the heat source, and as long as you baste frequently. The basting liquid should be largely fat or oil.

■ warm the basting oil or marinade because a cold liquid added to broiling meats will slow the browning.

■ rub surfaces of a broiler–pan or grill–with vegetable oil before you place the meat or chicken on it. This will prevent sticking and also make cleaning easier, especially for barbecue grills; rub them well with vegetable oil before you use them.

BROTH: see SOUPS AND STOCKS

BROWN SUGAR: see SUGAR

BRUSSELS SPROUTS
■ people who say they don't like Brussels sprouts usually have had them overcooked. Cook Brussels sprouts for about 10 minutes, rarely more, so that they'll retain their greenness when served.

BUNS
■ to reheat breakfast buns (especially cinnamon buns, which are usually quick to harden), put a pan of hot water in the oven while they heat. This will soften them up.

BUTTER
■ see also *Oleomargarine.*
■ one reason for buying sweet butter rather than salt butter is that salt can disguise off-flavors. Salt butter can be a little rancid without its being detected. This is not so with sweet (unsalted) butter. For this reason, sweet butter is often stored more carefully, and is apt to be fresher.
■ to make your own butter, pour pure, heavy, untreated (not ultrapasteurized) cream in the blender and whip until butter forms. This takes a very short time. You may need to turn the blender off and push the cream down against the blades once or twice. Then scrape the butter onto a piece of

kitchen muslin, fine cheesecloth, or large white handkerchief, and squeeze to drain out the moisture. If you don't want sweet butter, add a little salt. Pat into a bowl and chill.

■ to cut serving slices from a standard stick of cold butter, put the butter wrapper itself around the knife blade and you'll make nice clean cuts, without sticking.

■ to soften ice-cold or frozen butter quickly, grate it with a coarse grater or against the underside of a strainer with large holes and leave it at room temperature for a few minutes. It'll be just right for creaming with sugar to make a cake batter, for example.

■ to make browned butter, be especially careful to heat the butter very slowly so that it browns evenly. To make butter quite brown, lift the pan from the heat every now and then, swirl it, and sniff it to be sure it isn't beginning to burn. Take care not to overdo it—if it burns, it's useless.

■ when melting butter over direct heat, it won't be as likely to burn if you add a little cooking oil. Be sure to keep the heat low.

■ to get packed butter or shortening out of a measuring cup, hold the lower part of the cup in a pan of hot water for only an instant.

■ for clarified butter (pure butterfat with none of the milk solids in it), use the following method, which is quicker and less messy than most: Put the butter in a small pan, then set the pan in a larger one containing hot water, and heat until the butter melts completely. Let the pan of butter cool to room temperature, and then refrigerate it. The pure butterfat will solidify and you can lift it off. (Don't throw away the white residue; it's full of protein and flavor. Keep refrigerated and add it to cooked vegetables.)

■ clarified butter can be heated to a higher temperature

than regular butter without burning because the milk solids have been removed.

- to make whipped butter at less than half the store cost, let a stick (½ cup) of butter come to room temperature, then whip it to lightness with an electric beater. Slowly, add 8 tablespoons of cooking oil, 1 at a time, beating well after each addition. After everything is well whipped, remove the mixture from the bowl with a rubber spatula and store in a container in the refrigerator. The volume of butter will have doubled. And it will stay spreadable even when cold.

- if you use whipped butter in baking (uneconomical, but sometimes there is no choice), weigh it, don't go by volume.

BUTTERSCOTCH BITS
- a 6-ounce package of butterscotch bits equals 1 cup.

CABBAGE

- when you choose winter cabbage, look for a tight, firm head. The exception is young spring cabbage, which is softer.

- it's likely that a cabbage is coarse and has a strong flavor if the stems of the outer leaves have begun to detach themselves from the main stem.

- an easy way to separate cabbage leaves to prepare stuffed cabbage or cabbage rolls is to wash, dry, core, and freeze the head of cabbage. Defrost it, and the leaves will separate easily.

CAKE

- see also *Baking Powder, Baking Soda, Blender, Cupcakes, Fats and Oils, Flour, Icing.*

- you can bake a 1- or 2-egg cake calling for 2 cups of flour or less in an 8-inch square cake pan, or in two 8-inch round ones. For every ½ cup of additional ingredients (flour, nuts, fruit, etc.), use a pan size that is 1 inch larger either in length or width, or use an additional smaller pan.

- grease the bottom and sides of a cake pan with shortening before you line the bottom with waxed paper. Then grease the surface of the paper, pour in the batter, and bake. With this method you can cool the cake in the pan and when you remove the cake, the waxed paper will stick to the pan rather than to the cake.

- to keep your hand clean when you grease cake pans,

slip it into a small plastic bag, dig out a bit of shortening, and grease the surface. You can replace the bag in the can to use the next time.

■ don't grease the pans you bake sponge and angel food cakes in.

■ You won't have to grease your fruitcake tin if you line the inside with brown paper. After the cake is baked, leave it in the pan on a cake rack to cool. Then remove the cake–the paper will pull off easily.

■ before you make an upside-down cake, line the pan with aluminum foil. Cool the cake for 10 minutes after baking, cover the top with a serving plate, invert, and peel off the foil carefully. The top of the cake will look unruffled and professionally baked.

■ when you bake chocolate cake or chocolate cupcakes, dust the greased pans with sifted cocoa. It adds to the looks as well as the flavor.

■ cakes containing molasses will be less likely to stick to the baking pan if you line the pan with waxed paper before pouring in the batter.

■ when you're using honey or molasses in a cake recipe, measure the oil or other shortening in the measuring cup first. Use the same cup for the honey or molasses, which will then pour out easily without sticking to the inside of the cup.

■ a square layer cake is nice for a change. Instead of pouring batter into traditional round pans, pour it into the 8-inch square ones that many cooks use for noodle or potato puddings. Or use a couple of loaf pans, taking care not to fill them higher than you would a cake pan. This will give you an oblong layer cake.

■ if you're going to sprinkle chopped nuts in a buttered pan before you pour in the batter or dough, butter the pan well, sprinkle the nuts over the bottom, and chill before pouring in the batter or dough. The nuts will adhere to the pan surface better.

MIXING

■ if butter is very cold (or even frozen) and you've forgotten to soften it to use in a cake batter, grate it with a coarse grater or against the underside of a strainer that has large holes and leave at room temperature for a few minutes. You'll find the butter just right for creaming with sugar.

■ it's much easier to cream butter and sugar together if you sprinkle a few drops of water over the mixture.

■ add all spices and flavorings, liquid or powdered, to the shortening when you begin to mix a cake batter. The flavors will be distributed more evenly throughout the batter.

■ you can make a pretty fair cake flour by substituting cornstarch and all-purpose flour. To get 1 cup of "cake flour," add 3 tablespoons of cornstarch to about ⅞ cup of all-purpose flour, then sift. This isn't perfect, but it can sometimes get you out of a hole.

■ for most cake batters, use 1½ teaspoons of baking powder for every cup of flour.

■ you can almost always substitute 2 egg yolks for 1 whole egg in a cake recipe.

■ when a recipe calls for egg yolks and egg whites to be beaten separately, always beat the whites first (it usually doesn't matter if they stand for a short time). Then you won't have to wash the beater before beating the yolks. If you beat the yolks first, you *do* have to wash the beater, because the minute any trace of egg yolk touches the white, you'll never be able to whip the whites to frothiness.

■ a quick way to mix cake and cookie batter and still get a light texture is to have a quart-sized screw-top jar handy for mixing all the dry ingredients. Shake everything up well and pour into the mixing bowl. Then use the blender to mix all the wet ingredients–milk, eggs, shortening, extracts, etc. After everything is thoroughly mixed, pour the contents into the bowl of dry ingredients and mix. In no time you've got your batter ready, and you'll be surprised at how fine the texture will be. (Keep the screw-top jar on the shelf with your other cake ingredients–there's no need to wash it each time you use it.)

■ you can prepare the dry and wet ingredients of a cake batter separately, ahead of time, well before you put them together to make your cake. Mix the dry ingredients in a screw-top jar and set aside until needed. The wet ingredients (milk, eggs, shortening, extracts, etc.) can be mixed in a screw-top jar and refrigerated for as long as 4 days before you use them.

■ if you have to make a cake on a day when you know you're going to be rushed, measure out all the ingredients the night before, refrigerating the wet ingredients. Then in the morning you can just go to it. This is a great time saver.

■ always insert the beaters in an electric cake mixer before you plug it in.

■ after you've finished beating a cake batter with an electric mixer, hold the beaters less than an inch above the batter and set the mixer at the lowest speed. Most of the batter clinging to the blades will spin off, and with little spatter.

■ don't overbeat sponge cake batter or it will lose its lightness. Mix thoroughly, but stop as soon as all the flour has been incorporated into the batter.

■ beat a couple of tablespoons of creamy peanut butter into the batter of a white or golden cake, then bake as usual.

■ the best fruitcake batters are very stiff. The right amount of liquid to use when you're making a fruitcake is only enough to allow you to mix the dough, with its burden of fruit, in the mixing bowl.

■ an angel food cake will be lighter and finer if you use superfine sugar. Or put the sugar in a blender for a few seconds at moderate speed.

BAKING

■ put your angel food cake in a cold oven–*then* turn on the heat. Try this method. It works!

■ cake pans shouldn't touch one another in the oven–or the oven walls.

■ if the surface of your cake seems to be browning too quickly, cover it lightly with aluminum foil for the last 5 minutes of baking.

■ if you have trouble with cheesecake cracking while baking, it may be because your oven was too hot. Another way to avoid this problem is to bang the pan gently several times on a level surface–after you've poured the cheese filling into the shell–to force out possible air bubbles.

■ a cheesecake should always cool to lukewarm in the oven with the door open. Then it should be refrigerated.

■ very few cakes won't benefit by turning the cake pan halfway around toward the end of baking. This allows all sides of the cake to get the same amount of heat.

■ most cakes should be cooled first in their pans. But a freshly baked cake removed from its pan won't stick to the cooling rack if you oil your palms with cooking oil and rub the surface of the rack.

SERVING AND STORING

■ a freshly baked cake can be brought hot and steaming from the oven and cut at once into individual portions and served as a pudding dessert. Pour any hot sweet sauce over it.

This is a good tip to remember for a cake that didn't quite make it, but is still edible.

- before you remove a cake from the pan to the serving plate, sprinkle the plate with a little granulated sugar. This will keep the cake from sticking to the plate.
- when you cut a cake with a knife, the pressure often causes the cake to mat. This won't happen if you get yourself a cake cutter, a metal gadget with a handle and a series of long tines. It's particularly handy for cutting angel food cake.
- or wash a serrated or straight knife blade in very hot water, dry it quickly, then slice.
- a cake will stay fresh for several days, especially if it's been cut, if you put half an apple with it and keep it covered.
- don't ice cake or coffee cake before you wrap and freeze it. Make the icing and freeze it in a separate container. Ice the cake after both the icing and the cake are defrosted. A coffee cake that's been frozen can be heated first, before icing. It will look and taste freshly baked.

CANDLES

- candles will burn more slowly and last longer if you put them in the freezer the day before they're needed. There's one caution, however. Very thick candles may crack when frozen. Put them in the refrigerator instead.

CANS AND CANNED FOODS

- see also *Muffins.*
- generally, canned goods stay wholesome for about a year, so it's a good idea to write on the cans the date you bought them.
- store canned foods in a cool, dry place. Cans rust in high humidity. Too much warmth may cause the contents to

deteriorate as the weeks pass. (Too cold isn't good either–if the contents of a can freeze, throw the can out.)

■ in an emergency, you can often use a clean can in place of a small pot on the stove or in the oven to heat food.

■ use cans for storing foods in the refrigerator or the freezer. Cover with aluminum foil and use stick-on labels to mark each can before storing. A word of caution: Don't save any cans for storing whose opened metal edges are jagged. Save only those cans that have perfectly smooth openings.

■ one reason cans are good for storage is that you can strain hot liquids or fats directly into them without fear of cracking or breakage. And when you freeze foods in cans, you can stand the cans directly in a pan of hot water to defrost the contents.

■ use the 4- or 6-ounce cans that mushrooms or tomato paste come in for freezing small amounts of rich stock to use in gravy or sauce, or for adding to soups. There's no need to thaw a large container of stock when you need only a little.

■ small-sized cans are also excellent for freezing egg whites, lemon juice, or individual portions of baby food that you've prepared.

■ for freezing individual servings for a meal, 8-ounce and 10-ounce cans are perfect. When the time comes for thawing and heating, put the can in a low oven or in a pan of water on the stove over low heat. You can sometimes stand a can directly on a very low burner. This usually works best for frozen liquids or foods that contain a good portion of liquid.

■ when you're heating an opened can of food in a pot of water, the can is likely to bounce around a bit unless you place something between the bottom of the pot and the bottom of the can. A good object to use is a flat key, the type that opens a sardine can.

■ the opened ends of clean cans make nice cookie cutters.

CANTALOUPE: see MELONS

CAROB: see COCOA

CARROTS

■ 1 pound of cooked carrots, drained and mashed, makes 1⅓ cups; 1 pound of raw carrots, grated, makes about 3 cups.

■ cooked mashed carrots can be used interchangeably with pumpkin in a recipe calling for mashed pumpkin.

■ small cooked carrots—or larger ones cut into 2- to 3-inch lengths and whittled a little to round the edges—make a lovely garnish. Butter them lightly and dust them with very finely chopped parsley.

CAULIFLOWER

■ some cauliflower come with lots of bright green leaves that make good eating. Blanch them lightly and serve with butter, or stuff them just as you would cabbage leaves.

■ cauliflower will stay white and taste sweeter if cooked in half milk and half water without a cover. Or cook it in milk alone. (Use the milk for a sauce or as the base for a cream soup.)

■ don't discard cauliflower stalks when you cook the head (or curd). Trim off the dry, fibrous parts, blanch, and cut up to serve cold in salads. Or cook them, cut into strips or slices, and serve with a white or hollandaise sauce.

CELERY

■ 1 large stalk of Pascal, or green, celery, diced, will give you about ¾ cup.

■ Pascal celery contains more vitamin A than white celery.

■ you can stuff celery with practically any sandwich spread or cracker dip.

CEREALS

■ if you have some dry cereal that doesn't seem to be getting used up, pulverize it in the blender and use with appropriate seasonings—instead of bread crumbs or flour—to sauté fish, croquettes, etc.

■ leftover cooked cereal can be chilled, cut in slices, and sautéed like scrapple. Dip the slices in beaten egg and crumbs first. This can be a very healthful starch substitute at a meal. (And it really tastes good.)

CHEESE

CHEDDAR CHEESE

■ 4 ounces of grated Cheddar cheese will give you about 1 cup.

COTTAGE CHEESE

■ 1 cup of creamed cottage cheese weighs about ½ pound.

■ cottage cheese is made from skimmed milk, but most has some cream and a little rennet added.

■ store containers of cottage cheese upside down in the refrigerator so the cottage cheese will stay moist.

■ pot cheese is a nonfat, no-salt cottage cheese that has had much of the moisture pressed out.

SERVING

■ cream cheese and cottage cheese are wonderful spreads

for hot waffles, or pancakes. You can sprinkle brown sugar over the cheeses, or use them with fruits or syrups.

STORING

■ you can freeze an unopened package of cream cheese. When thawed, it's not quite as smooth-looking as before, but it's perfectly good and tasty for all cream cheese uses.

■ most firm cheeses will keep easily for 2 months in the refrigerator if bought fresh and kept unopened in the original wrapping.

■ the best way to store an opened piece of cheese in the refrigerator is to use a jar—one with an opening large enough to accommodate the width of the piece of cheese. Set the cheese, standing up, on the inside of the jar lid, then invert the jar and screw it onto the lid. Store in the refrigerator, lid end down. You have an airtight and odortight covering. And you can see what's in the jar.

GRATING

■ before you grate cheese, brush a little oil on the grater with a pastry brush. It will be easier to wash afterward.

■ stand a wide-mouthed funnel in a tall glass or jar and grate the cheese into it. This will prevent the cheese from flying out every which way as you grate.

■ if you don't have a grater, you can scrape Romano or Parmesan or any other hard cheese with a 4-tined fork.

■ if you need to grate or shred a very soft cheese, try putting it in the freezer for about 30 minutes first.

■ if you freeze Roquefort, blue, or Gorgonzola cheese, it will grate very nicely into a salad dressing or into any dish calling for finely crumbled cheese.

■ any dried-up cheese (Swiss, American, Cheddar, etc.) can be grated and used over vegetables, soups, etc.

■ another use for dried-up cheese is to cut it into small chunks and put the pieces in the blender with some slices of raw onion and add some sour cream or yogurt. This makes a marvelous canapé or sandwich spread.

COOKING

■ Italian Fontina cheese melts more smoothly and is less stringy than mozzarella.

■ for a cheese sauce that won't curdle, first make the sauce without the cheese. When the sauce is cooked and nearly as thick as you want it, fold in the freshly grated cheese. Don't boil the cheese sauce after this step.

CHEESECAKE: see CAKE

CHERRIES

■ a pound of fresh stemmed cherries will give you about 3 cups; pitted, about 2½ cups.

■ a paper clip makes a great cherry pitter. Open it out into a hook and use it to pierce the cherry and push the hook under the pit. Just give the clip a twist and with the other hand pinch just behind the pit. It comes right out. And it's fast.

CHESTNUTS: see NUTS

CHICKEN

■ see also *Leftovers, Stuffing*.

■ when you buy a whole chicken, count on ½ pound per person.

■ 2 pounds of unboned chicken breasts will give you about 1½ pounds of meat after boning.

■ a fowl (older chicken) costs less per pound than a

young chicken for frying or broiling. An older bird also has a lot more meat on it and will taste just as good as a young one.

PREPARING
- don't leave chicken in its plastic wrap when you store it in the refrigerator, or after it's been defrosted. It will develop an unpleasant odor. Wrap it loosely in waxed paper or a damp dish towel, so air can get to it.
- you can marinate an older chicken so that it's as tender as a young one. Use a warmed mixture of oil, wine, and herbs. Pour this over the bird and let stand for about 4 hours at room temperature, turning now and then. You can also marinate it in the refrigerator for a day. You'll be surprised at how tender the chicken will be.
- a rather tough chicken can also be tenderized if you marinate it overnight in the refrigerator in nothing more than seasoned white wine or dry vermouth.
- an old bird can also be made tender by long gentle simmering. Stew a cut-up bird in about 3 cups of water with any vegetables and flavorings you like. Cover and simmer—never boil—for a couple of hours. The chicken will end up very tender indeed.
- it's much easier to bone chicken breasts if you freeze them slightly.
- chicken halves will broil evenly if you split the meat partway at the leg joint where the thighbone and backbone meet.
- rub the entire surface of a chicken with a little salad dressing (this can contain a little mayonnaise if you like) before you put the bird in the oven. It's not only tasty, but it also keeps the chicken moist.
- if you like Southern-style fried chicken, don't dry the

chicken pieces after you've washed them. Roll them in a mixture of 1 cup seasoned flour and 1 teaspoon of baking powder.
Fry in 1 inch of hot fat.

▪ you can make a flour coating for chicken crispier and
lighter if you mix a little cornstarch well into the flavored flour
(about 2 teaspoons of cornstarch to ½ cup of flour).

▪ to get a crisp, dry coating on chicken, sauté the pieces
(turning them once) only enough to cook slightly. Put them
in the oven to finish cooking and browning.

▪ you can get a nice cracker crumb coating on fried
chicken by dipping the pieces in evaporated milk before rolling
them in the cracker crumbs. Let stand about 10 minutes before
frying or sautéing.

COOKING

▪ to sauté coated chicken pieces quickly and still get a
crusty skin, cover the pan during the first half of the cooking. If
you like a tender skin, cover the pan during the last half of the
cooking.

▪ the dark meat of a chicken has more flavor than the
white. If you're adding pieces of chicken to a soup, it will have
a richer taste if you include a lot of the dark meat (drumsticks
and backs).

▪ chicken gizzards are the toughest part of a chicken. By
cutting them in pieces and simmering until tender in a little
liquid or stock, you can shorten the cooking time if you are
using them in a stuffing or for a fricassee.

▪ if you don't eat chicken skins, freeze them. When you
have enough, simmer them in lightly salted water for an hour
to make the greatest chicken broth ever. (You can remove the
fat after cooling.)

CHILI SAUCE: see KETCHUP

CHOCOLATE CHIPS
- a 6-ounce package of chocolate chips will give you 1 cup.

CHOWDER: see SOUPS AND STOCKS

CINNAMON: see HERBS AND SPICES

CLAMS: see SHELLFISH

CLARIFYING
- you can clarify hot fat, consommé, broths, etc., very easily by letting them drip through a paper coffee filter that has been fitted into a funnel with a narrow neck.

CLEANING TIPS
- keep a small soaped sponge near the stove to wipe up grease spatters and avoid bigger cleanups later.
- a toothbrush is ideal for cleaning a strainer, scrubbing a grater, cleaning the blades of a blender, and a dozen other kitchen uses. Keep one near the sink.
- keep some coarse sand handy. It's marvelous for scouring the insides of bottles you can't otherwise get at. Fill the bottle about a quarter full of sand, add a little soapy water, screw the cap on, and shake like crazy. Pour the contents into a strainer, then rinse the bottle and the sand well. Let the sand dry and store it again for future use.
- or you can tie tiny pebbles or coarse sand very loosely in a small piece of nylon stocking knotted at both ends and use to clean a bottle or jar. Shake well with soapy water and you'll see the inside of the bottle get clean as a whistle. Pull out the knotted stocking, rinse under running water, and hang it up to dry.

- if you want to keep your drinking glasses absolutely free of marks, dry them with a dish towel in each hand so that your fingers never touch the glass.
- those flat, green sheets of hard sponge that are meant for cleaning cars without scratching the finish are good for scrubbing enameled pots and nonstick-coated pans. They're like nonscratching scouring pads. Cut the big sheet into handy-sized pieces—6 inches by 3 inches, for example.
- don't throw away those plastic mesh bags that onions and potatoes often come in. Use them to put soap ends in. Cut the bag to size, knot the ends, and you've got something with which to wash dishes and scrub things. (These mesh bags are also handy for drying vegetable pieces and mushrooms in.)
- put soap ends in a quart container half full of water and keep adding bits of soap as they're left over. In time you'll get a thick, soapy fluid that is great for certain cleaning chores. For example, you can use it for cleaning a jar or bottle you can't get your hand into. Fill a jar or bottle with the fluid and let stand overnight, then pour the soap back into the storage container and rinse the jar or bottle with hot water. It almost always comes out sparkling clean.
- when you have to clean a doughy or floury counter top, or any surface made messy by food preparation, dust it first with salt. The flour or food remnants will never stick to the cloth or sponge when rinsed out.
- perform potentially messy food chores in or over the sink: measuring flour, pouring soups and sauces from pots into other containers, flipping eggs or omelets. If you should have an accident, think of the cleanup work you'll be spared.
- to freshen smelly household sponges, soak them for several hours in a solution of 2 tablespoons of baking soda to 1 pint of water.
- to make your kitchen smell nice (or to cover up an

unpleasant odor), put a teaspoon of whole cloves and a slice of orange rind in a cup of water, bring to a boil, then simmer for 10 minutes.

COCOA

- cocoa is chocolate with most of the fat (cocoa butter) removed.
- add a tablespoon or two of strong coffee to your hot cocoa. Good!
- some people can't eat chocolate or cocoa. They can try a substitute, however. Use carob powder in place of cocoa in any recipe for cakes, cookies, or brownies. Carob powder is available in many supermarkets. Use the same amount of carob powder as you would cocoa, but cut down a little on the sugar called for in the recipe because carob powder contains some natural sugar.

COCONUT

- when you're picking out a coconut, look for a heavy one that sounds full of liquid when you shake it.
- once a coconut is opened it won't keep for much more than a week in the refrigerator, but you can freeze the pieces. They'll be less likely to dry out if you submerge them in coconut milk and store in containers.
- to remove the coconut meat from its hard shell, cover the pieces with boiling water and simmer for 8 to 10 minutes.
- if you want freshly grated coconut, cut the coconut meat into small pieces and drop them in the blender. This is easier than—and every bit as good as—grating the pieces by hand.
- don't throw away shredded coconut if it begins to dry out. Toast it by spreading it on a cookie sheet, and heat in a

moderate oven. Shake the pan occasionally so the coconut browns evenly. Use as a dessert topping on cookies or sprinkled over a cake icing.

COFFEE
- 1 pound of coffee, brewed, will give 40 to 50 cups.
- if you have to buy coffee for long storage, buy whole coffee beans. They oxidize less rapidly than ground coffee. (See *Blender.*)
- use the blender to grind your own coffee. Freshly ground coffee is much more flavorful than ready-ground.
- after you've opened a can of coffee, keep it in the refrigerator rather than on your pantry shelf. (If you don't use it up quickly, keep it in the freezer.)
- unopened cans of coffee will retain their flavor longer in the freezer.
- for drip, percolator, or vacuum-type coffee makers, use 1 heaping tablespoon of ground coffee for each ¾ cup of cold water.
- even though many fancy coffee makers are on the market, you might discover that boiled coffee can give you a first-rate cup of java. Use the finest grind. You'll not only get a delicious cup of full-flavored coffee, but you'll also find it economical—no need to use a full coffee measure per cup of water. A little more than half a coffee measure (the equivalent of 1 rounded tablespoon) is enough for 1 cup of rich boiled coffee.
- and here's how to make boiled coffee without any fancy paraphernalia: Put ground coffee and cold water into a pot, allowing a few inches at the top so the contents won't boil over. Bring to a rolling boil and remove the pot at once from the heat. Allow it to quiet, then return it to the heat once more. As soon as the coffee starts the second boil, remove the

pot from the heat and let stand for about 1 minute. Then pour into cups. There's no need for a strainer because after the second boil the grounds always sink to the bottom.

- coffee that has overboiled and become bitter (though this shouldn't happen) can be made palatable if you add ¼ cup of club soda to each 1 ½ measuring cups of hot coffee. Stir well.

- it may surprise you to learn that regular instant coffee (not decaffeinated) contains quite a bit less caffeine than the equivalent amount of regular brewed coffee.

- mix regular coffee with an equal amount of decaffeinated coffee and you can halve the amount of caffeine you take in—and still get the taste of coffee.

- the nearest thing, in taste, to brewed coffee is freeze-dried coffee. In freeze-drying, the coffee bean isn't heated as long as regular instant coffee. (But freeze-dried coffee is usually more expensive than regular instant coffee.)

- if you're going to serve coffee in demitasse cups, you can use regular coffee if you make it half again as strong as you usually do.

- make frozen cubes of very strong coffee; put a couple in a cup and pour boiling water over them. You have instant real coffee.

COLLARDS
- you can use collard greens for rolling and stuffing just as you do cabbage. And you don't have to blanch the collard greens first as you do with cabbage: Just wash, fill, and roll. They'll soften properly during the cooking.

COOKIE SHEETS
- don't knock yourself out to scour cookie sheets. They do a better job of baking cookies when they're not shining and

gleaming. As long as they're clean, you can forget the baked-on stains.

COOKIES

- see also *Cupcakes, Fats and Oils, Nuts.*
- you can often make cookies using a recipe for cake dough: Eliminate practically all of the liquid from the cake recipe and use only half as much baking powder as the recipe calls for.
- if you use cooking oil instead of solid shortening in cookie dough, the cookies will be more tender. Conversely, a solid shortening makes cookies crunchy.
- put ¼ cup or so of almonds, pecans, or walnuts in the blender, grind them quickly to a rather coarse powder, and add to the cookie batter. Use a little less flour than the recipe calls for. Whoever eats these cookies is in for a delight.
- whole bran and wheat germ are nutritious and economical substitutes for nuts in cookies.
- if refrigerator cookie dough seems a little too soft to form into cylinders, don't be tempted to add more flour to stiffen it. Instead, stick the bowl of dough in the freezer for about an hour. You'll find the dough easier to handle.
- to form refrigerator cookie dough into cylinders, push the dough into long, narrow cans that have had both ends removed. Store these in the freezer (for future use) or the refrigerator. Use cans from concentrated frozen juices or the elongated cans asparagus, etc. comes in. Save one end of the can. When you're ready to slice the dough into cookies, push in at one end of the can with the can end. Slice off the dough at the other end as thin or as thick as you like. Use a cheese cutter or a buttered knife for this.
- almost any cookie dough makes a dandy pie pastry,

especially for open-faced tarts, etc. Knead the dough a little, roll it out, and fit it into a pie pan just as you would pastry dough.

- the opened ends of clean cans make neat cookie cutters.

- here's a suggestion for cutting out cookies: Roll the chilled cookie dough between 2 sheets of waxed paper and slip this into the freezer for 15 minutes. Remove, pull off the top sheet, and cut out the cookies.

- to flatten thick drop cookies before baking, slip a piece of nylon stocking over the bottom of a glass. Dampen the stocking and use to tamp down the cookies to the thickness you want.

- cookie batter thins and spreads out on hot cookie sheets, so either cool the cookie sheets before you use them again or have an extra one that can cool while the other is in the oven.

- if you let brownies cool completely in the pan before cutting them, you'll be able to cut the squares neatly without tearing.

- cookies made with oil will keep for at least 2 weeks in a cookie jar. But butter cookies, unless you freeze them, will develop an off-flavor after a week.

- cookies that have become hard can be softened if you store them for a day or so in a closed container with half an apple.

- you can also soften cookies that have become too crisp or dry by storing them overnight in an airtight jar with a slice of fresh bread.

- if you make cookies with honey instead of sugar, you'll find them at their best about 2 weeks after you bake them. They ripen. Store the cookies, separated by squares of waxed paper, in closed jars in a cool place.

- a quick way to put a nice topping on cookies without

making an icing is to cover the cookies with jelly or preserves before you bake them. The cookies, when cool, will have a tasty glaze on them.

■ whip an egg white lightly, then brush it over the cookies and dust with granulated sugar before baking. This gives a shiny sweet crust to the cookies.

COOKING FOR ONE

■ if you live alone and don't enjoy having to create daily menus for yourself, a freezer can be your best friend. Cook for four, or any number in a particular recipe. After cooking, save one serving for immediate eating and freeze the other servings, wrapped individually (see *Cans and Canned Foods* for how to make this easy). You'll not only eat well, but also spare yourself from cooking three other separate meals.

■ if you don't drink much milk, but use only a little in your coffee, you can still buy it by the quart and not worry about its going sour. Pour the quart of milk into 3 or 4 small bottles or jars with good screw tops. Allow a couple of inches of room for expansion on freezing. Set them in the freezer. (Milk defrosts at room temperature in a few hours, and perhaps a day in the refrigerator. If you want to hasten thawing, stand the bottle or jar of milk in a pan of cold water and shake the bottle or jar now and then. Once thawing starts, you can add a tiny bit of warm water to the pan. Let it stand and again give the bottle or jar an occasional shake. The milk will thaw in less than an hour.)

■ buy a pound of good steak—the very best quality, if you like—and divide it into thirds. Eat a portion the day you buy it—or the day after—and wrap and freeze the rest. (Unless you weigh over 150 pounds or are engaged in strenuous physical work, this amount of meat is all most people need at a meal.

Eat plenty of vegetables with it.) Out of that pound of steak you've got three meals for a moderate cost.

COPPER

■ if you're out of copper polish, dissolve a scant tablespoon of salt in ⅓ cup of vinegar, dip a soft cloth into the mixture, and rub the copper surface. Rinse well and dry. This really does the job.

■ or you can do a great job on copper by rubbing it with a piece of well-salted lemon rind. This works on brass, too.

CORKS

■ an easy way to get a cork out of a wine bottle is to dip a cloth in near-boiling water and quickly wrap it around the neck of the bottle near the cork. Then insert the corkscrew. The hot cloth will make the glass expand just a little.

CORN

■ a 1-pound can of whole kernel corn, drained—or a 1-pound can of creamed corn—will give you about 2 cups.

■ 5 to 6 ears of fresh corn will give you about 3 cups of kernels when cut from the cobs.

■ to remove the silk from an ear of corn, wipe downward toward the stem end with a clean damp cloth.

■ refrigerate corn as soon as possible after it has been picked. Corn begins to lose sweetness immediately, at room temperature.

■ like eggs, ears of corn toughen with overcooking. Depending on freshness, 5 to 12 minutes is usually enough. (Older ears tend to need slightly longer cooking.)

■ an old-fashioned method of cooking corn on the cob is

to cook it in half milk and half water. It helps to keep the corn tender.

CORNMEAL
- cornmeal won't form lumps if mixed well with a little cold water before you add it to any hot or boiling liquid.

COTTAGE CHEESE: see CHEESE

CRACKERS
- when crackers get limp, crisp them in a preheated 300° F oven for about 5 minutes.

CRANBERRIES: see BERRIES

CREAM
- cream for whipping should be heavy cream. If you can, avoid containers labeled ultrapasteurized or whipping cream. They contain additives such as algin and monoglycerides—substances no one needs in pure heavy cream.
- most of the "whipped cream" that comes squishing out of a nozzle is part air, part added chemicals, and—I suppose—part cream. Avoid it like the plague.
- keep heavy cream refrigerated until the very last minute before you whip it. The colder the cream, the easier it is to whip and the less likely it is to turn to butter during energetic whipping.
- whipped cream is easier and faster to make if *everything*—the cream, bowl, and beaters—has been chilled. This is especially true in a warm kitchen, where the cream is likely to turn to butter before it's thickened. You can also set the whipping bowl in a bowl of ice cubes as you whip.
- the best way to eliminate spatter when whipping cream

is to start out slowly. If you're whipping by hand, save the frenzy for later when the cream begins to thicken. If you're using an electric mixer, don't turn it up to whipping speed until the cream starts to thicken. Once thickening begins, there's very little spatter. This method may take a little longer, but you don't have to wash your walls afterward.

▪ if you plan to serve whipped cream over a sweet dessert, don't add sugar to the cream when you whip it. It's often not necessary, and the contrast can be delightful.

▪ never pour whipped cream on a hot dessert before you serve it; the cream will liquefy. Instead, serve it at the table.

▪ here are a couple of uses for whipped cream that may not have come your way. Mix a little into the juices of stewed or sautéed mushrooms, fold in the mushrooms, and serve. Also, whip and lightly salt some heavy cream and beat into hot mashed potatoes.

▪ you can freeze heavy, medium, or light sweet cream, but you can't freeze sour cream. It becomes liquid and will not thicken. (You can, of course, still use sour cream that has been frozen in cooking.)

▪ use sour cream (plus ¼ teaspoon of baking soda) to replace the water or milk in bread dough. It will give you a very tender loaf.

CREAM CHEESE: see CHEESE

CRÊPES

▪ crêpes, which you can freeze (stored between layers of waxed paper), sometimes crack in the freezer when they're laid flat. Try rolling them instead. Arrange the crêpes in layers of 3 or 4 with waxed paper between each crêpe, roll, and snap a rubber band around each roll. Store in the freezer. Crêpes thaw nicely at room temperature without breaking.

CRUMBS AND CRUMB CRUSTS

■ see also *Pies*.

■ 15 graham crackers pounded to fine crumbs will give you 1 cup. For coarse crumbs, 12 graham crackers should do it.

■ 22 soda crackers pounded to fine crumbs will give you 1 cup.

■ cracker crumbs are quick and easy to make, and much less expensive than those you buy. Just throw some crumbled crackers into the blender and grind to whatever fineness you like. If you're going to use the crumbs as a coating for fried or sautéed foods, toss in some caraway seeds, or sesame seeds, or paprika, or herbs of any kind.

■ food to be floured or coated with crumbs for frying or sautéing should be allowed to stand at least 30 minutes after being dredged. The coating will adhere better during the cooking.

■ hard, dry cookie crumbs are delicious when mixed into a regular dough. They give the cookies a crunchy texture, rather like ground nuts.

■ if a recipe calls for graham cracker crumbs, it's usually advisable to crumble the crackers with your hands (or with a hammer over waxed paper) instead of in the blender. When the crumbs are too fine, they tend to "mat" and become limp when mixed with moist ingredients.

■ sometimes a graham cracker crust pie can be cloyingly sweet, especially if the filling is rich. When you make your crumbs, substitute ⅓ cup of soda cracker or saltine crumbs for the same amount of graham cracker crumbs. If you use saltines, omit the salt called for in the recipe.

■ an easy way to lay a crumb crust evenly along the bottom and sides of a pie plate is to press the crumbs down with another pie plate a size smaller.

CUCUMBERS
■ when picking out cucumbers, choose the smaller, thinner, greener ones. Large thick cukes, and those showing much yellow on the surface, tend to be pulpy and tough inside and full of large seeds.

CUPCAKES
■ to make cupcakes all the same size, use an ice-cream scoop or a quarter measuring cup to ladle out the batter. For large-sized cupcakes, use a half measuring cup.
■ fill cupcake tins about ¾ full.
■ to make cupcakes into cookies, cut the cupcakes crosswise with a sharp knife after they're thoroughly cooled. Cover the slices with icing.
■ moist, crumbly cupcakes are often hard to remove from their tins. Set the cupcake pan in the freezer for a couple of hours and the cupcakes will ease out nicely with the help of a knife.

CURRY: see HERBS AND SPICES

CUSTARD
■ see also *Pies*.
■ the term *boiled custard* is a misnomer. A custard shouldn't really boil. If it does, it's likely to scorch. Keep at a simmer.
■ to make a custard with eggs rather than cornstarch or flour, the ratio should be 1 egg or egg yolk to every ½ cup of liquid. With this rule, you can make varying amounts and sorts of pie fillings, custard desserts, and vegetable quiche-type dishes. Add solids as you wish.
■ if you've made a custard that won't thicken properly—

never mind the reason – must you pour it down the drain? Not on your life. Pour the custard into a bowl and put it in the freezer. Take it out after an hour or so and beat it. Return to the freezer. After a couple of hours, remove from the freezer and beat it again. What have you got? You've got a pretty decent ice cream, that's what.

- you can also use an undercooked custard or a custard that won't thicken properly to pour over a pudding or ice cream.

- to see if a baked custard is done, insert a knife blade near the edge of the custard (not in the middle). If the knife comes out clean, the custard is done. The middle part of a baked custard firms during cooling. Remove a baked custard from the oven as soon as it passes the knife blade test. If a baked custard "weeps" or is runny, you've probably baked it too long.

- when you serve baked caramel custards, you can make sure the caramel is liquefied and flows nicely over the un-molded custards if you make the custards a day ahead and let them chill in the refrigerator until the time of serving.

CUTTING BOARD

- brush cooking oil over the surface and sides of a new wooden cutting board and let it stand for about a week. If dry spots appear on the board (this means the oil has seeped into the wood), put more oil on it. Wipe the board with paper towels and it's ready for use. Repeat this every 6 months or so and the board will not warp or split. (Never let a cutting board soak in water.)

- if possible, position your cutting board so it overhangs a table or counter top slightly. This arrangement comes in handy when sweeping peelings and other odds and ends straight into the garbage. (And the food itself, which you've cut on the board, can be swept into a dish or pot.)

D

DEFROSTING: see FREEZER AND FREEZING

DESSERTS

- see also *Cake, Custard, Ladyfingers, Pies.*
- the fillings of many pie recipes can be baked as is without a crust. Many of these baked fillings can be cut into wedges and served; others can be treated as hot puddings to be served with a spoon, and topped with anything you like.
- for an unusual dessert, freeze washed and drained berries in a flat serving dish, then at serving time remove from the freezer and pour cream over them. The cream will freeze slightly to the berries. The combination is wonderful.
- if you've made a fancy gelatin or similar kind of dessert that you'd like to arrange on a serving plate in advance, unmold the dessert hours earlier and invert a large bowl over it. Keep it chilled and safe in the refrigerator.

DISH TOWELS

- to quickly cool any cooked foods (boiled potatoes, asparagus, broccoli for salad, etc.), spread them out on a dish towel.
- small terry cloth hand towels are less expensive than terry cloth dish towels, although they're about the same size. In fact, the hand towels are usually more attractive. So the next

time you need terry cloth dish towels, try the linen department instead of kitchenware. And look for white sales.

■ if you have a few badly stained cotton or linen dish towels that have had their day, don't use them as rags—yet. Save these old dish towels to wipe off chicken and meats before cooking them. Toweling is much better than paper towels for this chore. Dish towels are also great for cooling freshly baked cookies on, or for the quick drying of mushrooms.

■ if you have an old, worn linen table cloth, consider cutting and hemming usable parts of it for dish towels. Real linen dish towels cost a bundle these days, and in any case it takes months of use before new linen dish towels become soft and absorbent. You can use parts of soft cotton tablecloths, too. Age lends cotton a wonderful absorbency.

DOUGHNUTS

■ to make firm doughnuts, refrigerate the dough for 8 to 12 hours before you form and fry the doughnuts. Put only a few doughnuts at a time into the hot fat to prevent the temperature of the fat from suddenly cooling. Fat that's too cool results in greasy doughnuts.

■ add a good-sized piece of stick cinnamon or 5 or 6 whole cloves to the cooking fat to give your doughnuts an interesting flavor. Of course you can always add a little ground cinnamon, cloves, mace, or nutmeg to the dough when you're mixing it.

■ if you've made more doughnuts than you can use right away, freeze the leftovers. Be sure to wrap them airtight. And don't ice them first. Thaw, then crisp them lightly in the oven before icing them.

DUCK
- 1 duck will serve 2 people.

DUMPLINGS
- when you drop dumplings into a pot of liquid, don't crowd them. Put in only enough to cover the surface without causing others to submerge.

EGGPLANT

- a 1-pound raw eggplant, diced, will make about 2½ cups; and 1¾ cups cooked.

- avoid eggplants that are wrinkled or dull-looking. They're likely to be limp and pulpy inside. Be sure the skin is tight and shiny.

- try to use eggplant within a couple of days after you buy it. If refrigerated for more than 3 or 4 days, eggplant loses flavor.

EGGS

- here's a fair rule of thumb for telling old eggs from fresh ones: The shells of old eggs tend to become shiny and smooth; fresh eggs have a rough, chalky appearance.

- some recipes call for beaten eggs and others call for unbeaten eggs. The addition of beaten eggs produces lightness in a batter; and unbeaten eggs make the ingredients adhere to one another (as in meat loaf).

- if you've overfried an egg and no one will eat it, just mince it up, add a little mayonnaise, and you've got egg salad for a sandwich.

- an egg glaze (for painting the surface of unbaked bread, pie, or any pastry before baking) is made by beating 1 egg with 1 teaspoon of water. This gives a shiny, brittle crust.

- a tablespoon of sherry does wonders for scrambled eggs and omelets. Beat it into the eggs before you cook them.

■ butter or any kind of fat should be heated to the bubbling point before you add the eggs.

SEPARATING

■ chill eggs before you separate the yolks from the whites. Yolk membranes are firmer in chilled eggs and are not as likely to break.

■ if you have trouble separating eggs, you might try breaking them, one at a time, into a narrow-necked funnel. The yolk will remain above and the white will slip through.

■ when separating the yolk from the white, there's no better method than to make a bowl of one hand and pour the raw egg gently into it. The yolk will stay in your hand and the white will drip through your fingers. It doesn't take long to master this simple technique. And you don't have to worry about breaking the yolk, as occasionally happens when you shift the egg from one half shell to the other. Those shell edges are sharp.

■ when a recipe calls for egg yolks and egg whites to be beaten separately, always beat the whites first (it usually doesn't matter if the whipped whites stand for a short time). Then you won't have to wash the beater before you tackle the yolks. If you beat the yolks first, you *do* have to wash the beater because the moment any trace of the yolk touches the white, you'll never be able to whip the white to frothiness.

■ if you've separated an egg and see a bit of yolk in the white, remove the bit of yolk by touching it lightly with a moistened cloth.

OMELETS

■ eggs served as a main dish are a bargain when you compare their cost with that of meat. For example, make a main dish of a 2-egg omelet per person. Fill the omelets with pieces of leftover meat, chicken, or vegetables, in fact anything you have on hand. To make a filled omelet, beat the eggs with a little water or milk, add pepper and powdered garlic, then pour into a hot greased pan as you would any omelet. After the eggs have lost most of their runniness, pour the filling, which should be heated separately, on top. With a spatula, roll half the omelet over on top of the filling, heat for 15 seconds, and ease out of the pan onto a warm plate. With potatoes and salad on the side, you've got a filling and healthful meal.

■ for another delicious omelet, add a well-rounded teaspoon of sour cream for each egg you use. Whip well into the eggs.

■ for an interesting omelet variation, have ready a sauce of some kind—a white sauce seasoned any way you like, or a gravy with chopped vegetables or bits of meat in it. Make the omelet as usual and after it's done pour the sauce over it, then pop it under the broiler for about 1 minute. As soon as the sauce sizzles and begins to brown, ease the omelet onto a plate and serve right away.

■ if you like your omelets fluffy, beat in ¼ teaspoon of cornstarch for each egg you use.

BOILING

■ it's important to know that eggs begin to cook while the water is heating, so if you time eggs from the point at which the water reaches a boil, the smaller the amount of water you use, the more accurate your timing will be. Use only enough water to just cover the eggs.

■ to ease the shelling of hard-boiled eggs, put a tablespoon of vinegar in the water in which you boil them. After they're cooked, crack them gently all over and they'll practically leap intact out of their shells. (Even cold hard-boiled eggs are easy to peel if boiled in water with vinegar.)

- cold hard-boiled eggs are easier to slice without crumbling than hot eggs. If you need sliced eggs for sandwiches, or for a garnish, etc., hard-boil, peel, and refrigerate them for a few hours before slicing.
- if it's important to you that the yolks of hard-boiled eggs be exactly centered (in making stuffed eggs, for example), stir the water from time to time while the eggs are cooking.
- a pastry blender is a quick and efficient tool to use for mincing hard-boiled eggs for egg salad, etc.
- another way to prepare eggs for mincing is poaching instead of hard-boiling them. You won't have to bother with peeling the eggs and it's quicker. If you poach the eggs in broth, they'll have more flavor.
- for very good stuffed eggs, mash the hard-cooked egg yolk with a little anchovy paste. Set a small sprig of parsley in the center of each stuffed egg.
- it's hard to tell a hard-cooked egg from a raw one on the refrigerator shelf. If you think the problem will come up, add ½ teaspoon of turmeric or some beet juice to the water in which you cook the eggs.

EGG WHITES
- 1 egg white equals about 2 tablespoons.
- egg whites will beat up more quickly if you add a pinch of salt to them.
- if you lift the beater up and down occasionally while mixing egg whites, you'll get more frothiness. This method incorporates more air into the mixture during the beating process.
- freeze egg whites in ice cube trays if the trays have individual plastic cups that hold one ice cube each. Pour one egg white into each cup, slide the tray carefully into a plastic bag, and set it in the freezer.

■ when you use an egg white to clarify broth or con-sommé, take care not to overbeat it. Egg white should be beaten only until it begins to froth, before adding to the broth or consommé.

■ here are some uses for leftover egg whites, besides the traditional fruit whips, angel food cakes, meringues, etc.:

CHICKEN OR FISH

■ cover cooked chicken or fish with a well-beaten me-ringue into which you've whipped a couple of teaspoons of sour cream and any herbs you like. Then dust lightly with grated cheese and paprika, and pop into the oven or under the broiler until lightly browned.

COOKIES

■ substitute 2 egg whites for 1 whole egg in a cookie recipe. You'll get different, but good cookies. Or whip an egg white lightly, then brush it over the cookies and dust with sugar before baking. This gives a shiny sweet crust to the cookies.

MACAROONS

■ these are variants of baked meringues, with ground nuts and a little flour and flavorings added.

MARSHMALLOW SAUCE

■ this is often what you end up with when you bollix up a meringue by adding the sugar too soon. But it's great over puddings, cake, or ice cream. Spice up the sauce with cin-namon, nutmeg, or vanilla.

MAYONNAISE

■ you can make a pretty fair mayonnaise by substituting a couple of egg whites for egg yolks.

EGG YOLKS

▪ the color of an egg yolk depends on what the hen was fed. It has nothing to do with the nutritional value or age of the egg.

▪ to make egg threads to blend into a soup, Chinese style, heat a little butter in a pan. When the butter begins to bubble, pour in 1 or more egg yolks that have been beaten with a little cold water. Immediately tilt the pan so the yolk mixture coats it entirely–the thinner the better. As soon as the sheet of yolk is lightly cooked (no longer runny), turn it out on a cutting board. Cut into very thin strips with a sharp knife. Add to a clear soup–any soup, actually–before serving. If you like, when you first beat up the yolks, throw in some finely cut chives, fresh dill, or parsley. Egg threads can turn a good soup into a memorable one.

▪ you can substitute 2 eggs yolks for 1 whole egg in a cake recipe. Add a little extra milk or other liquid.

▪ if you're going to store 1 or more egg yolks in the refrigerator for a few hours before using them, rinse the storage cup or jar before you slide the yolks in. A dry container is more likely to cause the yolk membrane to break.

▪ egg yolks can be frozen and thawed and used just as you'd use fresh ones. Mix ½ teaspoon of honey well into every 6 yolks before freezing and they'll thaw smoothly without forming a "skin" or becoming gluey.

ENERGY SAVERS

▪ when you're cooking something in the top of a double boiler, boil a few eggs in the bottom part for free. You can always use hard-boiled eggs for salads, sandwiches, etc.

▪ after you've finished using the oven, don't waste the accumulated heat. Slip a pan of diced or sliced vegetable bits into the oven to dry as the oven cools. This is a good thing to do with a leftover half onion or a couple of aging carrots. You'll have dehydrated vegetables for stews and soups that will cost you next to nothing. Be sure the oven isn't too hot, even though you've turned off the heat, otherwise the veggies may brown or char when what you want them to do is dry.

■ when you use the oven for any purpose—baking or roasting—sneak a cake or some cookies in. You can bake them for nearly free. While they're in the oven, adjust the temperature to suit them—the food you're roasting won't mind.

■ a stew or soup will generally continue to simmer on top of the stove for 10 minutes after you've turned off the heat, so you can lessen the amount of heat you use by this length of time. This adds up!

■ if you have a self-cleaning oven (which holds heat longer than a regular oven because of extra insulation), you can turn the heat off at least 10 minutes before the final cooking time, and the food will continue to cook.

■ defrost frozen foods before cooking and you'll shorten cooking time and energy used.

■ a good general rule for most top-of-stove cooking is to keep the heat as low as possible and still maintain the cooking. This saves money and energy, and lessens the likelihood of scorching.

FATS AND OILS

■ it may be economical to buy cooking oil in a 48-ounce bottle, but a bottle that size is unwieldy. So for daily use, pour some of the oil into 1-pint or even ½-pint narrow-necked bottles (use a funnel). Keep the large bottle on your storage shelf for refilling the smaller bottle as needed.

■ strain, cool, and refrigerate any fat or oil that you've used for frying or sautéing. Store it in a covered jar in the refrigerator or freezer. It's not only economical but it's also already flavored and you may need to add very little seasoning to what you're cooking when you use it.

■ you can substitute vegetable oil for solid shortening in much baking and general cooking. If you're making this substitution in a cake, cookie, or pancake batter, use 1 or 2 tablespoons less oil than the amount of solid shortening called for.

■ the temperature of hot fat has reached 365° F if a 1-inch cube of bread dropped into the hot fat browns in 1 minute.

■ never pour water or other liquids or wet foods into hot fat. The fat will rise and overflow and may very well catch fire. Furthermore, you might get burned. Also, never cover a pot in which you're deep-fat frying. The steam won't be able to escape and the result can be the same as adding liquid to hot fat: dangerous spattering.

■ you can make walnut-flavored oil rather inexpensively (real walnut oil costs a fortune). Toast ⅓ cup of walnut pieces in the oven or in an unoiled skillet until they're a little dark. Stir now and then—be careful not to let the nuts burn. Grind them in the blender with ½ cup of cooking oil and let them stand in a jar for a day or two. Strain the oil through several thicknesses of cheesecloth or through a white handkerchief. Use the oil in salad dressings or for sautéing. It's delicately flavored and delicious. Refrigerate it, and be sure to shake it well before use.

■ you can clarify hot fat by straining it through a coffee filter placed in a narrow-necked funnel.

FIGS

■ fresh figs don't keep well. Plan to eat them immediately after you buy them.

FISH

■ see also *Leftovers, Sauces and Gravies, Shellfish*.

■ very little fish odor will cling to your hands if you dip your hands in cold water before you handle the fish.

■ leftover cooked fish (salmon, halibut, etc.) can be frozen. When it's thawed it flakes as beautifully for a salad as freshly cooked fish.

■ cover frozen fish with milk and defrost in the refrigerator. Drain and pat dry before cooking. The flesh will be firmer and have a pleasant taste.

■ also, when you thaw frozen fish, don't thaw it completely before you cook it. The juices that are still partly frozen inside the fish will remain there when the outside is cooked, and the whole piece of fish will be moister.

■ you can make a chowder from canned tuna. Cook and dice some potatoes. Sauté diced onion, celery bits, and pieces of bacon together. Then combine all of these with milk and a can of tuna. It's a pretty good chowder.

■ the oil from canned fish can be very good for sautéing onions and other vegetables. You can also mix the oil
with lemon juice and a little pepper to make a fine salad
dressing.

■ don't soak or cook salt cod in metal bowls or pots. The
metal often discolors the fish.

■ for a variation on a butter sauce or a white sauce to be
served with fish, use white wine instead of milk and add a
teaspoon or more of prepared mustard.

■ a large number of fish and shellfish recipes are interchangeable. If a recipe calls for shrimp or lobster, you can often
substitute fish fillets. The cooking time may need to be modi-
fied, but the method and the sauces won't. The final dish is just
as delicious.

FRYING AND BROILING

■ when you fry or broil fish (this is true of meat, too),
add salt only after cooking. Salt pulls the moisture out of fish
(or meat).

■ for delicious fried or broiled fish, be sure that the fish
is thoroughly dry before you put it in the pan or on the
grill. (Use paper towels or paper napkins, pressing gently
to dry.) Coat the fish if frying; or brush with a little oil,
if broiling.

■ you can get a crunchy, cracker crumb coating on fish if
you dip the fish in evaporated milk before you roll it in the
cracker crumbs. Let stand about 10 minutes before frying or
sautéing.

■ you can make a flour coating for fish crispier and
lighter if you whip a little cornstarch into the flavored flour
(about 2 teaspoons to ½ cup of flour).

■ put a little ginger (powdered or fresh) in the oil in
which you sauté fish for a zippy flavor.

POACHING

■ in many dishes you can treat any white-fleshed fish fillets the same as you would crabmeat. Poach or sauté the fish gently; when cold, dice or shred. Serve with the same sauces that crabmeat recipes call for. You can also serve the diced or shredded fish hot with a sauce, or brown the fish under the broiler, just as you would crabmeat.

■ because it's difficult to remove the skin from a cooked fish after it has cooled, skin it immediately after cooking or poaching, especially if you're planning to serve it cold.

■ fish fillets won't curl when you poach them if you use a very sharp knife to lightly score a line down the side of the fish from which the skin has been removed.

■ when poaching fish, add some grated horseradish to the court bouillon (the flavored poaching liquid).

■ if you're poaching fish for no more than 4 people, use white wine and seasonings instead of water. (Poaching for more than 4 may require at least 2 bottles.)

■ never discard the liquid you poach fish in. If you're not going to boil the liquid down for a sauce—or if you have more than you need—freeze it and use it for poaching fish at another time. The liquid will get more and more full-flavored, and can be used in a fish chowder or as a base for fish sauce.

■ if large fish such as salmon and halibut have been properly poached, their flesh should be custardlike—not raw, and not dry and stringy from overcooking.

FISH STOCK

■ use all the fish bones you can get your hands on. Ask your fish store to save you the carcasses of flounder, sole, haddock, etc., after the fillets have been cut from them. Fish bones make the most splendid stock imaginable. And save the remains, including bones, of any fish you serve. They're still full of flavor. If you're not ready to make stock right away, freeze the bones in a plastic bag until you are.

FLOUR
- see also *Blender, Thickeners.*
- 1 pound of sifted all-purpose flour makes about 3½ cups.
- 1 pound of sifted cake flour makes 4½ cups.
- whole wheat flour can be made lighter and more delicate for use in cookies and cakes if you sift it. Use the finer sifting for the cookies and cakes, and add the coarse siftings, which remain in the strainer, to the flour you use for baking bread.
- instead of sifting white flour, pour it into a screw-top jar and shake briskly before you measure out the flour. For a cake or pancake batter, measure flour into a jar, then add baking powder, salt, and the other dry ingredients. Shake and pour. Quick, and no mess.
- unbleached white flour can remain good for up to 2 years if stored well wrapped and kept fairly cool.
- store all-purpose flour in huge glass jars with wide mouths and screw tops. Shake the jar before sifting the flour. Also, measuring from a jar is easier than having to monkey around with the paper bag that flour usually comes in.
- you can make a decent oat flour for baking bread by putting uncooked oats in the blender and running it until the oats are finely ground. You can also use oat flour in pancakes, muffins, and waffles.
- it's very easy to measure out cake flour if the flour is stored in a large round box that oats come in. Before measuring the cake flour, shake the box up and down briskly, then give the flour a minute or two to settle. The cake flour is now sifted—it doesn't need to be put through a sifter or strainer.

FRANKFURTERS
- we tend to forget, but years ago a frank wasn't just slapped into a roll and handed to us. The roll was *toasted* and *buttered* first. Go thou and do likewise.

FREEZER and FREEZING
- see also *Bananas, Cooking for One.*
- overripe fruits and vegetables are not good for freezing, so be sure that any fruits and vegetables–from your garden or store-bought–that you intend to keep in the freezer are not too ripe.
- any fresh vegetables, fruits, herbs, etc., that you intend to freeze should be as dry as possible before you wrap them to put in the freezer.
- if you're freezing food you've already cooked, store it in cans. Cover the cans with aluminum foil, label them, and stick them in the freezer. When you want to defrost a can of food, the quickest method is to stand it in a pan of water and heat it up–no worry about scorching. You can pour the contents of the can straight into a serving dish.
- the waxed cardboard containers that milk and cream come in are also handy for freezing foods–especially stock, soups, etc. Wash and dry the containers before use. When you're ready to remove the frozen food, tear the carton apart and discard it.
- put a piece of waxed paper under any container placed in the freezer and the container will never stick to the freezer shelf. This is particularly good for anything that has a moist bottom, such as an ice cube tray.
- clear plastic shoe boxes are wonderful for freezer storage. Put *wrapped* meats, fish, chicken, or vegetables in them and label the side of the box that faces front. They're space-saving and can be stacked. One box can be used for small odds and

ends: Throw them all in, label the box miscellaneous, and save yourself a lot of rooting around in the freezer when, for example, you want that little jar of lemon juice or that egg white you froze for future use.

■ if you have an electric self-cleaning oven, defrosting your freezer is a cinch. Stash all the frozen foods in the oven and keep the door closed. A self-cleaning oven is usually so well insulated that it will keep even ice cubes frozen for a couple of hours.

FROSTING: see ICING

FRUITCAKE: see CAKE

FRUIT JUICERS
■ the type of hand juicer you turn a half of orange or lemon on to press out the juice should have a pointed cone, not a rounded one. You'll get more juice.

FRUITS
■ see also *Berries* and the names of individual fruits.
■ don't buy fruits because you like their shiny coats. These fruits are often covered with a thin coat of wax to make them more attractive. And some oranges are artificially colored. An intelligent consumer knows that true beauty is more than skin deep.
■ the syrup in which canned fruits are packed is often labeled light, heavy, or extra-heavy. These refer to increasing amounts of sugar in the liquid.
■ cereal will get less soggy if you put the sliced fruit or berries in the bowl *first,* then cover with the cereal.
■ fruits that are cut up for salad will keep their natural color if you sprinkle them well with lemon juice.

■ dried fruits will be less sticky to chop or cut if you freeze them first. And cutting will be easier still if you heat the knife or keep dipping it in hot water.

■ any fruit you eat, you can drink. All you need is a blender. Depending on the fruit, you can add water, milk, honey, lemon or lime juice, or anything else that appeals to you. Invent your own fruit punch.

■ frozen juices not only taste good but also are a healthful treat for youngsters. Pour the juice into 6-ounce paper cups and put them in the freezer. They're ready to eat, popsicle style, in a few hours: Push up on the bottom of the cup to use it as a holder.

■ put small cans of fruit juice in the freezer, and when they're frozen use them to pack with lunches that have to be kept cool. If packed in the morning, the cans will have served their purpose as "ice cubes" and be thawed by lunchtime.

■ you'll find that stewed fruits will need less sugar if you simmer the fruit for about 10 minutes before sweetening.

FUDGE

■ to cool fudge, spread it about ¾ of an inch thick in the cooling pan.

■ after being poured, fudge should cool for at least 30 minutes before being cut.

FUNNELS

■ every kitchen should have funnels of at least 4 neck sizes. Not only do jars and bottles have different sized necks, but some liquids, like soups, contain larger pieces of solids, and a wide-necked funnel does away with the painstaking transfer by spoon of these large pieces.

GARLIC

- pick heads of garlic that are hard to the touch. Soft, spongy garlic has lost much of its flavor and may be partially spoiled.

- the yellow, central strip of the garlic clove (the "lily") has the sharpest garlic odor and taste. Halve the garlic clove and you can remove the lily easily with the point of a knife.

- rub the inside of a cooking pan with half a clove of garlic if you want only the slightest hint of garlic in what you're cooking.

- before you put salad in a serving bowl, squeeze the juice of 1 clove of garlic into the bowl, or put the clove through a garlic press. In either case, rub the bowl thoroughly with the juice or the pressed bits before adding the salad. The garlic will be transmitted gently to the greens without over-powering them.

- garlic that is to be removed after you've used it in cooking or flavoring brine for pickles, etc., need not be peeled first. Wash the cloves, cut them in half lengthwise, and drop them in whatever you're preparing.

- you can peel a garlic clove easily if you first lay it on its side and swat it with the handle of a heavy knife.

- to make a pleasant garlic oil to use on meats or to rub on a chicken before roasting, add slices of garlic to cooking oil and heat gently until the garlic begins to darken. Immediately remove from the heat and strain.

■ a good way to store garlic for months in the refrigerator is to peel it, put it in a small jar, and cover it with salad oil. After you've used up the garlic, use the oil for sautéing or in salad dressing.

■ to grow garlic greens in your kitchen window, plant separate cloves of garlic in little pots and keep the soil moist. Each clove will shoot up greens that can be cut and used like chives. As you cut the shoots off, new ones will grow. And they'll grow for months. Garlic greens have a slightly milder flavor than the cloves.

■ you can make your own garlic powder at much less than the cost of buying it. Remove the skin from garlic cloves, cut the cloves into slices, and dry them thoroughly at room temperature. After the garlic slices have dried, pulverize them in the blender, or cover them with a piece of plastic wrap and pound with a hammer. Or use a mortar and pestle. Bottle the powder.

■ if you've overindulged in garlic and have become a social problem, eat a lot of parsley. It's a great tamer.

GARNISHES
■ see also *Hors d'oeuvres.*

■ garnishes are the little surface touches that can make a dish look more exciting and add that special something to its color, texture, and taste. Here are some techniques chefs use to give a touch of elegance to an ordinary dish:

ALL-PURPOSE GARNISHES
■ celery curls
■ celery stuffed with any minced or creamed mixture
■ finely chopped hard-cooked egg whites
■ hearts of celery

- pimientos sliced or finely diced
- radishes cut into thin slices or made into "roses"
- red or green peppers cut into thin strips or circles
- sieved hard-cooked egg yolks
- small pickled onions
- stalks of endive stuffed with cheese paste
- whole egg wedges

SOUPS

- chop a handful of almonds or toss them into the blender. These can be plain almonds, with their skins on, or blanched or toasted almonds. Each has a slightly different flavor, but they all look lovely sprinkled over a soup.
- cut scallion greens very fine, crosswise, into tiny green rings to float on soups.
- serve a dollop of faintly salted whipped cream on tomato soup or any creamed soup. You can dust the dabs of cream with paprika, curry powder, or finely minced chives.
- mix grated cheese and fresh parsley together in the blender. Dust the mixture over the top of a hot soup immediately after it's been ladled into bowls.
- float very finely shredded lettuce on a clear soup.

FISH AND SEAFOOD

- serve lemon slices, naturally—or lime. Better still, cut the lemons or limes into wedges to make squeezing easier. (Have you ever tried to squeeze a slice of lemon?)
- run some mayonnaise in the blender with a handful of chopped-up watercress to make the mayonnaise green and zesty. Put dollops here and there on the platter. You can also make pink mayonnaise by using a little tomato paste or ketchup.

- celery leaves, if they're bright green and fresh, are a delicious fish garnish. So is a handful of chives, finely cut, shaken from a spoon over the fish.
- cut stuffed olives in thin slices and arrange them, overlapping like fish scales, over part of the fish.

MEATS AND CHICKEN

- garnish any meat or chicken dish with tiny, white boiled onions (canned onions will do). Drain them well and heat in a little butter and honey until they're brown. They look and taste wonderful.
- throw some button mushrooms or mushroom caps into a pan with a little oil or melted butter and brown slightly. This doesn't take long if kept at a good sizzle. Sprinkle some paprika over the mushrooms and arrange them around a hot meat or chicken dish.
- you can do the same with orange sections, adding a bit of sugar to the hot oil or butter to caramelize the orange pieces a little. They send up a lovely aroma.

DESSERTS

- whole blanched almonds, or halves of almonds, for decorating cakes or puddings are tastier when dipped halfway in melted sweet or semisweet chocolate.

GELATIN
- 1 envelope of unflavored gelatin equals 1 tablespoonful.

GINGER: see HERBS AND SPICES

GINGERBREAD
- for a dark gingerbread, mix into the batter 1 table-

spoon of melted chocolate to each cup of warmed molasses called for.

GOOSE
- a goose has no white meat.

GRAHAM CRACKER CRUST: see CRUMBS AND CRUMB CRUSTS

GRAPEFRUIT
- 1 medium grapefruit will give you about 1 cup of juice.
- heavier grapefruit are usually juicier and have more meat.
- grapefruit, like oranges and lemons, should be open to the air during storage. Don't put them in closed bags or the skins will mildew.

GRAPES
- grapes are delicious when served slightly frozen. Put a bunch of seedless grapes in the freezer for about 45 minutes, then serve.

GRAVY: see SAUCES AND GRAVIES

GREEN ONIONS: see SCALLIONS

HAM

- run very hot water for a minute or two over a can of ham before you open it and you'll find the ham will slip out easily.

- to eliminate quite a lot of salt from thick ham slices used for sautéing, let the ham slices soak in water in the refrigerator for a day. Rinse and blot dry with paper towels before sautéing.

- an uncooked, smoked ham will stay fresh longer if you wrap it in a well-wrung-out cloth that has been saturated with vinegar. Then wrap the cloth-covered ham in waxed paper and refrigerate.

- before you bake a ham, make a lengthwise slit through the rind on the underside. Place the ham, slit side down, in the baking pan. After the ham is cooked, the rind will pull off easily.

HAMBURGER

- add some finely diced, lightly sautéed bacon to your hamburger mixture.

- ¼ cup of liquid to 2 pounds of meat is the right amount of liquid to add to hamburger meat to make it juicy for broiling.

- before you put hamburgers on a grill, coat the tops with any good spicy steak sauce or Worcestershire sauce.

- to make professional-looking hamburgers (and to

lessen the work), form the chopped meat into a cylinder of whatever diameter you wish. Roll the cylinder in plastic wrap or waxed paper and put it in the freezer for about an hour. Remove, unwrap, and cut into slices as thick as you like.

HERBS AND SPICES

■ if you're not familiar with certain herbs or spices such as cardamom, chervil, cumin, fennel, or mace, then become familiar–experiment. Take *one* of the many herbs and spices found on your market shelf and use it in the foods you usually cook. This is the best way to acquaint yourself, one at a time, with the magical flavors the rest of the world has discovered. You'll find your own favorites.

■ like all plants, fresh herbs contain a great deal of water. For this reason, the same volume of the *dried* herb has more herb essence and flavor. So when you substitute dried herbs for fresh, use approximately ⅓ of the amount.

■ herbs lose flavor when they get old. If you've had yours for some time, add a bit more than you would ordinarily to the dish you're preparing. And it's not a bad idea to note on the jar label the month and year you bought the herbs.

■ to freeze fresh herbs, wash and rinse them and then purée in the blender with a little water. Freeze the mixture as you would ice cubes, then store in plastic bags. You'll find these cubes fine and fresh tasting for soups, stews, or salad dressings.

■ you can buy a very expensive mixed spice-and-herb grind from France–or you can grind your own. Put a little of about a dozen different spices and herbs–whatever you've got on your spice shelf–in the blender, grind to a powder, and bottle. It's very good in omelets and cheese sauces–and in gravies, too.

■ keep a few little jars of herbs and spices already mixed with salt and pepper near the stove.

- whenever possible, buy whole rather than ready-ground spices (allspice, cardamom, cinnamon stick, cloves, nutmeg, pepper), and grate or grind them yourself. You can often use the blender for this, or a mortar and pestle, or a pepper grinder. You'll get much more pungency and flavor.
- to measure herbs, pepper, and other spices you're going to grind, do the grinding over a piece of waxed paper. Curl the paper and pour into a measuring spoon.
- to store your fresh herbs at summer's end, mash them up in some butter or oleomargarine and freeze them. These deliciously flavored spreads will last for months.

ANISE
- when you're using anise seeds in a cake, pudding, or other dish, crush the seeds first for maximum flavor. Do this between sheets of waxed paper with a rolling pin.

BASIL
- to use basil in pesto sauce, see *Sauces and Gravies.*
- use fresh basil leaves in salads.
- fresh basil will keep aromatic and green at room temperature for weeks in a glass of water. Change the water daily.
- if you grow basil in your garden, dig up some of the plants in the fall and grow them inside in the kitchen in a sunny window. You can have fresh basil through much of the winter.

CARAWAY
- caraway seeds are marvelous in a creamed soup. Simmer a tablespoon or two of the seeds in a clear soup stock for about 15 minutes before adding the milk or cream. Strain out the seeds, discard them, and continue with the soup as you nor-

mally would. Don't cook the soup for too long after this, or you'll lose the subtle caraway flavor.

CINNAMON

- add ¼ teaspoon of cinnamon to any rich pan gravy to serve over meat, chicken, or rice. This is common in Near Eastern cookery—and should be universal.
- add cinnamon to any rice dish—not just rice pudding—for wonderful flavor.

CLOVES

- to give doughnuts a lovely flavor, drop 5 or 6 whole cloves in the fat you fry them in.

CORIANDER

- coriander is a dark-green, pungent herb that is delicious cooked in a fish or meat sauce. It is also known as Chinese parsley.

CURRY

- curry powder is generally a combination of the following ground seeds and herbs: cardamom, cayenne, chili pepper, coriander, cumin, fenugreek, ginger, and turmeric.
- you can add a little curry powder to almost any soup (especially creamed or puréed soups).
- a little curry powder added to a meat or chicken gravy will lift it to another plane. The gravy then becomes a vehicle in itself: Add some sautéed onion, diced fruit (apples or mangoes are the usual, but any will do), and pieces of chicken or meat. Heat all this up and serve with rice. It's a fine way to use leftovers. In fact, curry powder was invented for leftovers. It will go with anything: birds of any kind, fish, meat, seafood, vegetables.

■ and don't forget eggs: Add a little curry powder to mashed hard-boiled egg yolks when you make stuffed eggs. Add it also to omelets or to scrambled eggs.

■ sauces made with curry powder become "hotter" when they stand. So, if you don't intend to eat a curried dish as soon as it's made, go a little easy on the amount of curry you use.

DILL

■ pound 2 teaspoons of dill seed and mix into the dough of a white or whole wheat bread.

GINGER

■ fresh ginger root isn't always easy to find, and it can be expensive. But you can grow your own in the kitchen. Place a piece of the root that contains a bud in a pot of soil. The root will send up shoots and leaves, and when the plant later becomes dormant and the shoots die off, you'll be able to dig up half a dozen or more new large roots (actually, rhizomes) to use in cooking—and to start new plants.

■ grate a little fresh ginger root into a salad dressing and shake well.

MINT

■ fresh mint leaves are great breath sweeteners. Chew a few.

MUSTARD

■ plant mustard seeds (the same kind you use in pickles, etc.) and grow mustard cress on your kitchen windowsill. The seeds will sprout in less than a week. Use the tiny leaves in salads, sandwiches, or any dish in which you use watercress.

PAPRIKA

■ to make your own paprika, dice sweet red peppers, dry them thoroughly, and grind to a powder in the blender. Or cover with plastic wrap and pound with a hammer. You'll get a deliciously pungent red powder which, although not from the same variety of pepper as the commercial paprika, has all the qualities of paprika—and tastes fresher. Furthermore, you can make a mild or tangy paprika. For a mild flavor, remove all the seeds and the white pith before you dry the peppers. If you like it tangy, leave the seeds and pith in when you set the peppers to dry, and grind everything together.

PARSLEY

■ eat the parsley that comes as a garnish with your meal. It's full of vitamins A and C—and is also a fine breath freshener.

■ you can keep fresh parsley green and crisp in the refrigerator for at least 2 weeks if you wash it and dry it thoroughly (roll it in a dish towel to dry). After it's clean and dry, put it in a screw-top jar and refrigerate.

■ a fast way to mince parsley very fine is to cut the leaves from the stems and discard the stems. Force the leaves into a tight ball, and holding the ball firmly with one hand, slice down through the ball of leaves with a sharp knife, working from the outside inward and making the slices very close together.

■ use a full-leaved sprig of parsley for brushing or sprinkling flavored oil or melted butter on fish or vegetables.

PEPPER

■ green peppercorns have a stronger flavor than white or black ones.

■ white pepper is black pepper with its outer shell removed. It's slightly less spicy than black pepper.

HONEY

- see also *Cake.*
- cakes and cookies made with honey keep much longer than those made with sugar and remain pleasingly moist. You can substitute ¾ cup of honey for 1 cup of white or brown sugar in baking, but reduce the liquid in the recipe by ¼ cup for every ¾ cup of honey you use.
- you can get a potful of unusual honey without having to shell out a potful of money. Slowly boil 1 cup of honey with ½ teaspoon of ground cloves. Cool the mixture before serving. It's great on waffles or ice cream.
- honey and corn syrup can be used interchangeably in baking.

HONEYDEW MELON: see MELONS

HORS D'OEUVRES

- see also *Garnishes, Leftovers.*
- you can make remarkably good pâtés or other spreads for canapés, etc., with meat or vegetable leftovers. Put them in the blender with a little butter or oil, possibly some sour cream or cream cheese, or anything spreadable you like. Spice it up plenty. People will beg you for the recipe.
- to make your own canapé crackers, cut thin-sliced white bread into rounds with a cookie cutter. Either toast the rounds lightly or butter them and cover with a topping that can be lightly broiled.
- put half a lemon or lime, cut side down, on a plate and stud it with the party picks your guests will need for spearing. This is very handy and looks pretty.
- to blend the ingredients in a spread or a dip for appetizers, refrigerate the spread or dip for a couple of hours before serving.

■ use cookie cutters on bologna, cheese slices, chicken loaf, sliced meats, etc., to make a fancy-looking platter of cold cuts. Grind the scraps to use in a pâté.

HORSERADISH

■ mix grated horseradish with finely minced, cooked or pickled beets. A delicious relish.

■ if you make your own grated horseradish (mixed with vinegar), store it in dark glass jars or in jars covered with brown paper. Horseradish tends to turn a grayish color when exposed to light.

■ grated fresh horseradish mixed with applesauce is a great accompaniment to beef and pork dishes as well as cold leftover meats.

■ a little grated fresh horseradish is wonderful for flavoring a fish sauce. And, used sparingly, it can be added to a salad dressing, too, especially for a coleslaw or chef's salad dressing.

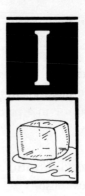

ICE CUBES

- ice cubes tend to splinter and become slightly hollow if they stay in the freezer too long. This can be avoided if you slide the trays into long plastic bags and twist the ends closed. Safe from the air, they won't lose moisture.

- plastic egg cartons can be used for ice cube trays.

- you won't have trouble with ice cubes getting into the spoon when you ladle punch or sliding out the spout of a pitcher if you make the cubes giant size. Use ½- to 1-cup size plastic containers.

- you can also make ice cubes in muffin pans or small empty cans. And you can get all kinds of odd shapes if you use éclair tins, ladyfinger pans, madeleine pans, etc.

- if you need ice cubes for their cooling action in picnic baskets, etc., freeze water in plastic containers with covers (leave room for expansion when you fill them). If the covers fit tight, you won't have any trouble with leakage. And the melted water can be drunk.

- fold a linen towel and sew up both sides to make a "bag" in which to store ice cubes. Empty the cubes directly into the linen bag and store in the freezer until you need them. They won't stick together.

- strong lemonade frozen in ice cube trays can be used in all sorts of drinks, including iced tea.

ICES

■ when making sherbet or ices, leave the mixture in the mixing bowl (with the beaters of your electric mixer, too) and put the whole thing in the freezer. In this way, when you have to beat the mixture again, there's none of the mess that usually results when it is removed from the freezer tray. Also, when both bowl and beaters are cold, whipping and thickening are quicker.

ICING

■ warm the milk before you add it to confectioners' sugar and you won't have lumps.

■ when a cooked icing is left standing for a while, it often "sugars." If this happens, beat into it ½ teaspoon or so of strained lemon juice.

■ to get an icing to whip up thick, put it in the freezer until it's very cold – then whip it.

■ if you're making a creamy fudge icing that doesn't stiffen after beating 15 minutes, whip in a teaspoonful of confectioners' sugar and let it stand for a little while. Then continue to beat the icing. And if the icing becomes too stiff to spread, add a teaspoonful of cream and beat some more.

■ to put the finishing touches to an iced cake, dip a broad-bladed knife in cold water and smooth the icing over the cake. The wet blade will keep the icing from sticking to it.

■ you can make a pleasing and quick cake icing out of mashed bananas. Add a little soft butter, lemon juice, cream, and some confectioners' sugar to the mashed banana, and mix well.

■ you can make a super-quick, delicious (and fattening!) icing by beating heavy cream until it's thick, adding a little vanilla extract, and finally, enough well-sifted confectioners' sugar to make the icing easy to spread.

■ for a quick white glaze on sweet rolls, brush the tops before baking with an egg white that has been lightly beaten with a tablespoon of milk. Sift sugar over this. If you want a yellow glaze, mix an egg yolk with the milk and dust with sugar.

■ a fine peanut butter icing can be made with very little fuss. Mix peanut butter, honey, and a little butter or oleomargarine until you get a spreadable mixture. Spread this over a hot baked cake while it's still in the pan and stick it under the broiler until the top sizzles. Then let the cake cool.

■ when you're icing cookies, place them on cake racks that have been set on waxed paper. Scoop up the icing that spills on the paper and return it to the icing bowl. There's no waste—and you don't have to be unduly careful about applying the icing.

■ the amount of icing it takes to fill and cover a 9-inch, 2-layer cake will usually cover about 2 dozen cupcakes.

■ if you have to cover an iced cake with plastic wrap, oil the plastic wrap lightly before you put it on the cake. This will keep the icing from clinging to the wrap when you remove it.

■ store leftover icing in a plastic container in the freezer. Keep adding any leftover bits of icing until you have enough for a cake. Never mind if the colors are different—add a little sifted cocoa with a tiny bit of warm milk for blending and you have a quick chocolate icing.

■ a good substitute for icing is a combination of cinnamon and sugar (1 tablespoon of cinnamon mixed with ½ cup of granulated sugar). Sprinkle over cakes and cupcakes while they're hot.

■ another substitute for icing is to place a lace paper doily over the top of a slightly warm cake. Sprinkle finely sifted confectioners' sugar liberally over the doily, being careful to cover mainly the little openings. Then carefully lift off the doily.

JAM AND JELLY

- see also *Berries.*
- here's a swift and easy way to make "jam." Mash any kind of berries and add a little honey to them. Mix well. You can also cook berries, cherries, or other fruit with honey until thickened. Then mix well and refrigerate. Use within 3 weeks.
- if you have trouble removing the paraffin layer from the top of a jar of jam, try inserting a corkscrew carefully into the center of the paraffin.
- cooking fruit in a pressure cooker for making jelly will extract a great deal more of the juice than regular top-of-stove cooking.

JARS AND BOTTLES

- see also *Cleaning Tips.*
- before you refrigerate a jar of food that you intend to open within a week or so, loosen the cover. A cold jar can be difficult to open.
- put on a pair of rubber gloves to open a stubborn jar; it does the same job as a rubber jar opener.
- if you find it hard to remove odors from jars and bottles whose insides you can't get at easily, pour in a mixture of 1 cup of hot water to 1 tablespoon of baking soda. Let it stand for a few hours or overnight.
- don't pour very hot liquid into a glass container without first rinsing the container well in hot water. The thicker

the glass, the more likely it is to crack if it hasn't been properly heated first.

- here's how to get a bottle filled with water to empty quickly: Hold the bottle upside down with two hands and make a quick, circular, sweeping motion. This forms a whirlpool inside, and the water will drain out in no time flat.

- if your kitchen tools (wooden spoons, whisks, etc.) won't stand upright in a storage jar, put a handful of marbles in the bottom of the jar.

JERUSALEM ARTICHOKES

- there's really no need to peel Jerusalem artichokes (they're difficult to peel when raw and almost impossible when hot). Scrub them well with a brush and soapy warm water and rinse.

- but you can peel raw Jerusalem artichokes and use them sliced in salads. They taste very much like—and have the same texture as—Chinese water chestnuts.

KETCHUP

- an unopened bottle of ketchup or chili sauce will stay fresh for about 1 year. An opened bottle (which should be refrigerated) will keep its flavor and color for about 3 months.

- to get ketchup to flow from a freshly opened bottle, insert the blade of a table knife a couple of inches inside and run it around the neck of the bottle. Invert, and out the ketchup will come.

- before you throw away an empty ketchup bottle, pour in a little vinegar and oil, cover, and shake. Pour the mixture into your bottle of salad dressing.

KNIVES

- don't buy a knife sharpener that looks like a pair of wheels between which you insert the blade for sharpening. It sharpens a knife edge unevenly and in time will ruin a good knife.

- get a small steel or ceramic cylindrical knife sharpener instead. And every time you wash a knife, give it a few strokes on each side of the blade. Rinse the knife and put it away. This is how to keep your knives sharp all the time.

- after you've sharpened a knife, don't use it before you've washed it; otherwise tiny bits of steel dust could get in the food.

- some of our grandmothers used this effective method to sharpen knives. There's often a rough, unglazed ring on the underside of kitchen mugs or ironstone plates, and this makes an excellent surface against which to sharpen a knife. Hold the knife at an angle, just as you would with a cylindrical knife sharpener.

- a knife loses its sharp edge not from the actual cutting of food, but from contact with the cutting surface–cutting board, counter top, etc.

- fruits or other foods containing acid will blacken and discolor a carbon steel knife (and any food you cut with it immediately afterward), so wash the knife as soon as you've used it on acid-containing foods.

- if you keep your knives in a drawer, make scabbards for the blades by flattening the cardboard cylinders that come with rolls of paper towels.

- onions tend to become discolored when cut with a carbon steel (as opposed to a stainless steel) knife. This won't matter for onions intended for cooking, but you might prefer to use a stainless steel knife if you're slicing onion rings for salad, for example.

LABELS

- if soap and water won't scrub the labels off dishes, glasses, etc., try rubbing with nail polish remover (acetone) on a bit of rag. Lighter fluid is also good for this.
- read the weights on the labels of cans and jars. You should be interested in the drained weight, not the net weight, of most foods.
- self-adhesive labels are handy for labeling the contents of cans or jars for storage on the shelf, in the refrigerator, and in the freezer. They pull off easily, but they don't wash off.

LADYFINGERS

- if you're making a dessert that calls for ladyfingers (such as tipsy pudding) and you want them to stand upright around a glass bowl, butter the ladyfingers very lightly on one side, and press the buttered side against the glass. Then fill the bowl with the dessert filling called for.

LAMB: see MEATS

LEEKS

- put a couple of white leek bulbs in a pot of moist dirt. They will sprout green shoots that you can cut and use just as you would scallions.

LEFTOVERS

- see also *Blender, Hors d'oeuvres.*
- when you make something using egg yolks, you're left with the whites. And when you prepare a dish using egg whites, you're left with the yolks. Make a list of recipes using egg whites and another list for those using yolks. Similarly, some recipes call for ingredients you don't use every day, and you may be left with more than you needed. Make a list of dishes using these too, so you need never throw precious food away. Examples: sour cream, coconut flakes, heavy cream, cottage cheese–to name just a few.
- the greatest use for leftovers that has ever been invented is spaghetti sauce. You can start with either a basic tomato sauce or a white sauce. Chop the leftover meats, chicken, vegetables, or even fish and mix them into the sauce. Spice it up with condiments of any kind. Heat and pour over cooked pasta. What you have, friends, is a dish you'd pay a small fortune for in a good restaurant.
- and sandwich fillings! Put leftovers in the blender with a little mayonnaise and jazz up the mixture with some seasoning. You'll have a delicious sandwich spread.

BATTER
- leftover pancake or waffle batter can be beaten into a creamed soup or sauce or other creamed dishes. Or it can be used as the base for a cream sauce to go over vegetables, etc.

FISH
- leftover cooked fish can be put through the blender and made into a pâté, just as chicken or meat can. Add mayonnaise or other moisteners, herbs, and other flavors. Use for stuffing celery or eggs, or as a canapé spread, or for fish cakes.

MEATS

■ a substitute for hamburger in recipes: ground or chopped bits of leftover roast or steak or stew meat. The final dish will probably be better than if you'd followed the original recipe.

■ you can make remarkably good pâtés or spreads for canapés with meat (and vegetable) leftovers. Put the leftovers in the blender with a little butter or oil, possibly some cream cheese or mayonnaise or sour cream—anything spreadable. Spice it up plenty. People will ask for the recipe.

■ Use meat and vegetable leftovers in a stuffing for chicken or turkey; or for stuffing cabbage leaves, green peppers, or tomatoes.

■ any leftover chicken or meat, fish too, can be ground and mixed with dumpling batter to make the tastiest dumplings ever.

PICKLE JUICE

■ mix the juice with oil and make a salad dressing. Usually no other flavorings are needed for this zippy dressing.

■ slice fresh unwaxed cucumbers very thin and set them to marinate in the refrigerator for a couple of days in pickle juice. You'll have crisp pickle slices.

SALAD DRESSING

■ to make a delicious hamburger, mix leftover salad dressing into the meat. Leftover salad dressing is also good mixed with flaked fish or chopped hard-cooked eggs for a sandwich.

SOUP

■ pour the leftover soup with its solids into the blender.

Add curry and other seasonings, and blend. Then heat the thickened mixture. What you have is a very tasty curry sauce to serve over rice. And although it may not be Indian, curry sauce is also great over noodles.

VEGETABLES

■ cut up and serve with a cream sauce flavored with curry powder.

■ mince and use as a filling for stuffed eggs and stuffed peppers.

■ mince and use in an omelet.

■ mash and add to chopped meat for very juicy hamburgers.

■ make chowders and creamed vegetable soups; add to pancake batter; make fritters.

■ to rebake baked potatoes, dip them in cold water and put them in a 350° F oven for about 20 minutes. Or peel and slice and make hashed browns or mash them. Mashed baked potatoes with butter are what mashed potatoes are meant to be.

■ dice, dry, and bottle leftover vegetables to use in omelets, soups, stews, and dozens of other dishes. Dried vegetable bits are not storage problems.

■ don't be too wedded to printed recipes. Feel free to make substitutions when they seem sensible to you. For example, if a particular sauce recipe calls for steamed cauliflower bits and you have lots of celery on hand, use it instead. Carrots, pumpkins, squash, turnips—even potatoes—often can be used interchangeably from one recipe to another (the same is true of fowl, meats, etc.). In some cases you may have to alter cooking times a bit, but that needn't be a great hurdle. Use up what's on hand.

■ the midnight food snacker discovered long ago that

there are mighty few hot dishes that aren't also delicious cold. If you have part of a casserole or some cooked vegetables left from a meal, you don't always have to try to pretty them up for future heating—make them part of a cold smorgasbord.

LEMONS

- see also *Pies*.
- 6 average-sized lemons will give you a little more than 1 cup of juice.
- the heavier lemons are, the juicier and meatier they are.
- lemons should be kept open to the air during storage. Don't keep them in closed bags or the skins will mildew.
- like oranges, lemons with smooth skins have more juice than rough, thick-skinned ones.
- rough-skinned lemons, however, are much easier to grate than smooth-skinned ones.
- because lemons have probably been sprayed, it's safest to scrub them very well with a brush and use hot, soapy water. Rinse and dry before you use them.
- whenever you see lemons on special, buy them even though you may not need them immediately. Squeeze the juice out of as many as you like. Refrigerated lemon juice will keep its flavor for well over a week. Frozen, it will last for months. Divide the juice into small amounts and freeze separately in baby food jars, for example, leaving room for expansion. Lemon juice thaws very quickly.
- you can get a more lemony flavor if you don't strain the juice, just remove the pits. For an even stronger lemon flavor, peel the lemon, remove the pith and pits, and blender the lemon at high speed. You have a marvelous flavoring for cakes, cookies, puddings, and sauces.
- squeeze lemon juice into ice cube compartments for

freezing. When you need to add the juice of a lemon to a sauce, for example, drop in one of the frozen cubes. For a cold dish, defrost the cube before use.

■ after you have squeezed a lemon, instead of throwing away the lemon skin, cut it into strips and freeze. Lemon strips are handy for flavorings and in cakes, cookies, and puddings.

■ you can also freeze thin strips of lemon peel in ice cube trays, after pouring a little water over them. These make pretty ice cubes for many types of cold drinks.

■ it's easier to grate a lemon diagonally across the grater rather than up and down. The lemon will move more smoothly over the grating surface.

■ strong lemonade frozen in ice cube trays can be used instead of ice cubes in all sorts of drinks including iced tea.

LETTUCE

■ see also *Salads.*

■ leaf lettuce has more vitamins A and C than head lettuce.

■ the best way to wash a head of lettuce (also escarole and other greens that come in heads or bunches) is to fill a large bowl or pot with cold water and pump the head of lettuce, stem side up, up and down in it. Do this in a couple of changes of water if necessary.

■ you can stuff lettuce leaves the same way you can cabbage leaves.

■ crisp shredded lettuce can be substituted for shredded cabbage in coleslaw.

■ wash wilted lettuce in cold water, shake it fairly dry, cover, and put in the refrigerator. In about 12 hours the lettuce will have freshened up surprisingly.

■ the leaves of refrigerated lettuce will be less likely to

"rust" if you wrap the lettuce in dry paper towels before you refrigerate it.

LIMES

- like lemons, limes should be bought by weight. The heavier they are, the juicier and meatier they are.
- buy very green limes. These are the tart and tangy ones. Yellowish limes have less flavor.
- limes keep well in the refrigerator if you store them in a capped jar.

LIVER

- to grind raw liver, freeze it partially first. (Or, if it's already frozen, partially defrost it.) Semifrozen liver grinds without losing its juices. Cut it into strips and feed it into the grinder.

LOBSTER: see SHELLFISH

LOW SALT DIETS: see SALT

MACARONI: see PASTA

MARGARINE: see OLEOMARGARINE

MARINADE

■ prepare a marinating sauce for meat, fish, or chicken the day before you need it. This allows the flavors to blend and enhance one another.

■ there are two easy ways of marinating. One is to put the meat in a very large screw-top jar along with the marinade. Screw on the lid and let stand, inverting the jar from time to time.

■ the other method is to put the meat and the marinade in a large plastic bag that you can twist-tie closed. Put the bag in a bowl and turn it now and then.

■ most marinating is best if done at room temperature, except in very hot weather when you may need to set the bowl in the refrigerator for a few hours.

■ the larger the piece of meat, the longer the marinating time that is required. A leg of lamb or a large beef roast will benefit if marinated for a couple of days.

■ if the piece of meat to be marinated is very large, prick it with a sharp fork here and there to allow the marinade to penetrate the meat.

■ if you're marinating meat in a bowl, be sure the marinade covers the meat at least halfway. And turn the meat every few hours.

■ you can use almost any salad dressing as a marinade for ripe olives, fresh or canned mushrooms, and many vegetables (if you blanch them first), including cauliflowerets, green or yellow beans, green or red sweet peppers, and onions. Let them marinate in the dressing for a day or so.

MARSHMALLOWS

■ 16 marshmallows weigh about 4 ounces.

■ store marshmallows in an airtight container in the freezer to keep them from drying out.

■ marshmallows are easier to cut if you freeze them.

MAYONNAISE

■ see also *Blender.*

■ an unopened jar of mayonnaise will stay in good condition for about 8 months; opened (and refrigerated, of course), for from 4 to 6 months.

■ mix mayonnaise with some yogurt to make a zippy dressing.

■ you can also mix sour cream with mayonnaise to make a very smooth and delicate dressing. Mix well.

■ here are three ways to add variety to mayonnaise: Mix ground watercress or feathery dill into it for green mayonnaise; a bit of tomato paste for pink mayonnaise; and a little turmeric and a dash of curry powder for a tasty yellow mayonnaise.

■ commercial mayonnaises often tend to be on the sharp side, possibly because there's too much vinegar in them and vinegar is high in acidity. But the mayonnaise you make yourself can be extremely delicate, and less expensive. Many cookbooks contain recipes for making mayonnaise, and if you have a blender, it's a cinch. One hint: The best vinegar to use is rice wine vinegar, which can be bought at many supermarkets. It's also available at Oriental grocery stores and gourmet shops.

■ if for some reason the mayonnaise you make doesn't thicken properly, you can always beat an equal amount of commercial mayonnaise into it, put it in a jar, and refrigerate. Most store-bought mayonnaises can stand a bit of thinning and all of them benefit by being made more delicate.

MEASURING
■ an ounce of liquid equals 2 tablespoons.

■ the little plastic measuring cups that come with cans of ground coffee hold exactly 2 level tablespoonfuls.

■ to measure flour or sugar from a container into a cup, set the cup on a piece of waxed paper. Later you can easily pour the overflow back into the original container.

■ if a recipe calls for shortening plus honey, molasses, or syrup, measure the shortening first. Then use the same measuring cup, without washing, for the liquid sweetening. It will roll right out of the cup when you pour.

■ suppose your recipe calls for ½ cup of solid shortening. The easiest way to measure it is to fill half the cup with cold water first, then spoon the shortening into this, pressing down until the water reaches the whole-cup level. For a ⅓ cup of shortening, fill the cup ⅔ full of water, etc.

MEATBALLS
■ form raw meatballs around a cube of cheese—any kind of cheese—mozzarella, American, whatever you have on hand. Cook the meatballs as you usually do and they'll have soft, creamy centers.

MEAT LOAF

- a little grated raw winter squash or pumpkin is a fine extender for a meat loaf.
- substitute wine (white, red, or rosé) for the liquid called for in your meat loaf recipe.
- when you put a meat loaf mixture in its baking pan, be sure to press the meat down firmly (use the flat of your hand) so no air holes are left at the bottom.
- if you're using bread crumbs in a meat loaf, you're better off using soft crumbs rather than the fine dry ones used for breading. Your meat loaf will be moist and delicate.
- if you want meat loaf to cook faster than usual, fashion it into individual-sized loaves. Or cook it in cupcake tins.
- if you want to remove an entire meat loaf in one piece from the loaf pan, butter or oil the pan first and then put a wide strip of aluminum foil down the length of the pan, with an inch or so of the foil overhanging at each end. Butter or oil the surface of the foil too, then fill and bake as usual. Let the meat loaf stand for 10 minutes after removal from the oven. Loosen it from the sides of the pan with a knife and invert the pan over a plate. The whole loaf should come out neatly. If you're careful, you can turn the meat loaf again, top side up, onto another plate.

MEATS

- see also *Hamburger, Leftovers, Meat Loaf, Stew, Wine.*
- ½ pound of ground meat equals about 1 cup.
- if you have to store meat in the refrigerator a bit longer than you usually would, dust all the surfaces of the meat well with ground white or black pepper. Wipe the pepper off with a damp cloth when you're ready to prepare the meat.
- before you put any kind of meat in a grinder, cut it into pieces and freeze the pieces for about 30 minutes.

This cuts down on stringiness when you grind the meat.

■ some commercial meat tenderizers contain salt or monosodium glutamate. Since sodium draws the juices out of meat, it's not a good idea to use these products. Read the labels before you buy.

■ the tannin in tea is a remarkably good meat tenderizer. If you've bought a tough cut of meat that you're going to use for stew, cook it in a little strong tea for 10 or 15 minutes, turning it now and then before you put it in the stewpot. Flavor the tea with a little salt, pepper, garlic, or any seasoning you like and pour it into the stewpot. It will contribute very nicely to the gravy.

■ squeeze or rub the juice of a papaya over a tough cut of meat. The enzymes are an excellent meat tenderizer.

■ there are other ways to tenderize a tough (and therefore usually inexpensive) cut of meat: Marinate it; braise it (cook in a little liquid, slowly, for a long time); pound it with a heavy instrument, a pot cover, or a special mallet; serve it sliced across the grain of the fiber.

■ a large roast of any kind should always be removed from the refrigerator at least 2 hours (3 is better) before being cooked.

■ meats you intend to broil or roast will lose very little of their juices if you rub or brush the outsides with flavored or unflavored oil before (and several times during) cooking. The oil forms a seal that prevents loss of inner moisture.

■ meats will shrink less during browning if you start the browning slowly.

■ roast all meats in a slow oven to prevent them from shrinking and losing their juices.

■ once a cut of beef is halfway roasted (after the outside has become well-sealed by the heat and oils), baste it with a red wine. Burgundy is especially good for this.

■ braised meats will have a richer gravy if you use stock or wine instead of water during cooking.

■ when grilling or broiling meat, the longer you cook it the tougher it gets.

■ when you prepare a leg of lamb for roasting, make tiny gashes here and there in the fat. Press a small piece of garlic into each gash. The roast will taste heavenly.

■ leftover bits of pickled, corned, or smoked meats can be used as you would use crumbled bacon. Chop coarsely, and sauté in any fat or oil until crisp. These are lovely in omelets, salads, or spreads of any kind.

MELONS

■ a honeydew melon, if bought too green, will never ripen properly. Avoid any that are green, hard, and smooth.

■ a ripe and ready-to-eat honeydew melon has a light-yellow, velvety-feeling skin with a slight softening at the blossom end.

■ a ripe casaba melon is yellow in color (not greenish) and the blossom end should be a little soft when pressed.

■ unripe muskmelons (cantaloupes) will never get very sweet.

■ here are the best ways to tell when a muskmelon is ripe: The surface netting should be coarse-looking and grayish and the scar at the stem end should be sunken in a bit. Also, there should be a slight softness at the blossom end, and a sweet fragrance.

■ a ripe muskmelon will keep its sweetness if it's chilled as soon as possible after being picked.

■ an ice-cream scoop is great for removing the seeds neatly and cleanly from the cut halves of melons.

■ don't buy a watermelon if one side is pale green or

whitish—a sign that it was picked too green. It will never develop into a tasty melon.

▪ want to eat a slice of watermelon without washing your face? Make cuts an inch or so apart down the slice as far as the white part of the rind. Spread the ends of the slice apart and each "finger" of the melon will stand up for easy eating.

MERINGUES

▪ see also *Egg Whites.*

▪ meringue-topped pies should always be cooled at room temperature—not in the refrigerator. And keep them away from drafts, otherwise you're likely to get "tears" in the meringue. Once cooled, refrigerate.

▪ dip a knife blade in water and use it to smooth or shape meringues before you bake them.

▪ to give a delectable, thin, crispy surface to a meringue topping for a pie, lightly shake some sifted confectioners' sugar over the top of the meringue before you set it in the oven to brown.

▪ if you've made a meringue that won't thicken because you either added the sugar too soon or because a bit of egg yolk might have escaped into the whites when you were separating the eggs, you've at least got a marshmallow sauce. Add a little almond extract and use what you have as a sauce for cake, or pudding, or ice cream. (You might like it enough to purposely add sugar to the egg whites too soon so you can get that velvety smooth sauce again.)

MILK

▪ if you're not in the habit of using much milk, you still don't have to worry about part of it going sour. Divide each quart of milk into thirds. Keep ⅓ in the refrigerator, and pour the rest into small containers (⅔ full) and freeze. Each container will defrost in about 4 hours at room temperature and can be used like fresh milk.

■ if milk does begin to go a bit sour, no need to throw it out. Don't drink it, but it's safe to use in cooking. Use it right away in cake batter or cookie dough (add ½ teaspoon of baking soda to your flour), or in pancake batter. Or use it in recipes calling for buttermilk in a cooked dish.

■ if you need sour milk or buttermilk for a recipe and you don't have any, use equal parts of yogurt and regular or canned evaporated milk to make up the amount of sour milk or buttermilk called for.

■ when you're measuring skimmed milk powder, don't pack it down in the measuring cup; spoon it in lightly.

■ dry (powdered) milk, if very well wrapped, will stay fresh for a couple of years.

■ "scalded" milk is milk that has been heated until bubbles form a ring around the top. Heat no more than this, or you'll have boiled milk.

MINT: see HERBS AND SPICES

MOLASSES
■ see also *Cake, Gingerbread*.
■ if a pie filling contains molasses, use a deep-dish pan or even a cake pan to bake the pie in. Molasses usually bubbles high during baking and might run over. To be safer still, set the pan on a cookie sheet.
■ heat 3 parts molasses to 1 part butter for a very tasty spread for pancakes and waffles. This saves on butter as well as syrup.

MUFFINS
■ put ¼ to ½ cup of some whole grain cereal in the

blender and grind to a fine flour to use in place of an equal amount of the white flour when you make muffins.

■ you can make wonderful muffins using yogurt. Substitute the same amount of yogurt for the liquid called for in the recipe. Add about ¼ teaspoon of baking soda to the dry ingredients, mix, and bake as usual. You'll have deliciously fragrant muffins.

■ when you make yogurt muffins, use any commercial yogurt-fruit mixture. Stir the contents well so the fruit is evenly distributed. You'll end up with tender, fruit-flavored muffins.

■ make muffins with a surprise inside. Pour only half the batter into the muffin tins. Place in each a piece of apple, or a pitted cooked prune, or a piece of canned pineapple, or any fruit you have on hand. Pour the rest of the batter on top and bake.

■ with only one batch of muffin batter, you can end up with several kinds of muffins. Add chopped walnuts or pecans to 1 cup of the batter; add bits of fruit, like chopped dates, to another; put some cinnamon in another part of the batch, etc.

■ sweet muffins for dessert are a tasty, healthful, and quick substitute for cake. You can cut the muffins in half, frost them, and make miniature layer cakes.

■ whip up a batch of unsweetened muffins to serve instead of bread not only for breakfast, but for dinner, too.

■ it's not necessary to grease the entire inner surface of muffin tins, only the bottoms.

■ fill muffin cups about ⅔ full.

■ muffins, which bake best in a somewhat humid atmosphere, do better in electric ovens than in gas ones (see *Ovens*). If you're baking muffins in a gas oven, leave one of the muffin cups empty and instead of filling it with batter, pour hot water into it. Then bake.

- bake muffins in a preheated oven. They need a sudden blast of hot air to rise to their maximum.

- for a crunchy, sugary crust on muffins, sprinkle a little white or brown sugar over them before baking.

- if you have trouble getting muffins out of the pan because the bottoms stick, place the pan while it's still hot on a wet towel for about 30 seconds. Then it will be easier to remove the muffins.

- if you break apart muffins just baked and they show elongated holes running up to the top, you've probably over-mixed the batter. Remember next time to mix the ingredients *only* until everything is moistened—no longer.

- hollow out leftover muffins, heat, and fill with a creamed mixture of any kind. A great luncheon dish.

- to reheat muffins that have hardened, set a pan of boiling water in the heated oven before you put in the muffins. They'll become nicely softened.

- you can bake muffins (as well as small cakes) in small buttered or oiled flat cans such as tuna fish cans. And if you remove both the tops and bottoms of the cans, you can use the rings to bake English muffins in. (English muffins are actually cooked on a greased griddle on top of the stove. See recipes for English muffins or crumpets.)

- if you're going to freeze English muffins, cut or tear them apart, stack the halves one on top of the other, the cut sides up, in a long plastic bag. In this way, the halves won't stick to one another.

MUSHROOMS

- a 4-ounce can of sliced mushrooms, drained, will give you about ¾ cup.

- read the labels before you buy fresh packaged mushrooms. Some brands have been sprayed with sodium bisulfide to keep them white. Sodium bisulfide may not be harmful, but when the sprayed mushrooms start to age they become slimy-looking, unlike mushrooms in their natural state.

■ older and somewhat darker mushrooms are more flavorful than white, freshly picked ones. Mushrooms lose moisture as they stand, and their flavor intensifies.

■ don't wash fresh mushrooms before you store them in the refrigerator. Like berries, they should be handled as little as possible until you're ready to use them. If your refrigerator is properly cold and the mushrooms are dry, they should keep well for more than a week. When it comes to storing mushrooms, moisture is their enemy.

■ when you serve mushrooms as a vegetable, use the caps only and save the stems and peelings. You can freeze them or dry and bottle them, and use them in soup stock.

■ braised, stewed, or sautéed mushrooms are delicious beyond belief when you mix a little thick whipped cream into their juices and then combine with the mushrooms.

MUSKMELON: see MELONS

MUSTARD

■ Dijon-type mustards are stronger than the general run of mustards most frequently found on grocery store shelves.

NOODLES: see PASTA

NUTS
- see also *Oats, Peanut Butter.*
- buy nuts in the shell if you can, for breads, cakes, or just plain eating. They taste much better than shelled nuts and cost a great deal less. Nuts in the shell are in their natural state. Shelled nuts often have been chemically treated before packaging.
- nuts in the shell, if kept cool and dry, will last a year. If shelled, they should be kept cold and will stay reasonably fresh for 6 months. They will stay freshest if kept in the freezer.
- put ¼ cup or so of any kind of nuts in the blender, grind to a rather coarse powder, and add to cookie batter. Use a little less flour than the recipe calls for. Whoever eats these cookies is in for a delight.
- if you have some shelled nuts—not enough to use in a cake—grind or chop them and add to ground meat for hamburgers or meat loaf. Nuts are a delicious meat extender and more nutritious than bread crumbs.
- if you have a cake or cookie recipe that calls for nuts and you don't have any on hand, try using any crisp, small-grained dry cereal.
- if you're going to add whole or large pieces of nuts to

cake or pudding batter, heat the nuts in the oven a little first, and they won't be as likely to sink.

■ you can make interesting nut butters of all sorts in the blender–cashew, peanut, pecan, walnut, etc. You may have to add a little oil after you've ground the nuts as fine as possible because home blenders are not as powerful as commercial grinders, but the result is great. You might also want to add a little honey and perhaps a bit of salt, but it's not absolutely necessary.

ALMONDS

■ almonds used in cakes or other desserts will have much more flavor if you brown them first. Use the oven or a pan on top of the stove–stir and watch the almonds carefully.

■ you can substitute very finely ground almonds for almond extract in cakes, cookies, icings, etc. Two tablespoons of finely ground almond powder will give you the almond flavoring of approximately ¼ teaspoon of the extract.

■ split almonds immediately after you've skinned them, while they're still hot and wet. Hold the almond against the cutting board, the flat sides between your thumb and forefinger, and cut them in half lengthwise with a sharp knife. If you want slivered almonds, cut each half lengthwise into 3 or 4 thin strips.

■ don't blanch almonds you intend to serve salted because they taste better with their skins on. To prepare salted almonds, use a tablespoon of butter or oil to every cup of almonds. Melt the butter (or heat the oil) over moderate heat in a large skillet, and add the almonds when the butter or oil begins to bubble. Mix with a wooden spoon as they heat. When they begin to smell toasty, remove with a slotted spoon and sprinkle with salt and maybe a little curry powder.

BRAZIL NUTS
- Brazil nuts shell very easily if you put them in the freezer for 6 hours before you open them.

CHESTNUTS
- an easy way to shell chestnuts is to cut a cross on both sides of each chestnut, spread the chestnuts out on a wide pan, and sprinkle ¼ cup of water over them. Put them in a pre-heated very hot (450° F) oven until the shells open, about 20 minutes. Remove them a few at a time. They peel easily while they're still hot.
- whether you boil or roast chestnuts, the time to peel them is while they're hot.

PECANS AND WALNUTS
- 1 pound of pecan or walnut meats will give you about 4½ cups.
- for a marvelous ice-cream or pudding topping, combine chopped pecans or walnuts with honey.

OATS

- don't buy oats for long storage. They have a relatively high fat content and in time the fat becomes bitter. Use them within 3 months.

- to substitute oats for nuts in cookies, mix the uncooked oats with a little butter and brown lightly in the oven. They're crispy and tasty.

- if you start "quick oats" in cold water, you'll never have lumps.

OIL: see FATS AND OILS

OKRA

- you can pickle whole fresh okra just as you do small cucumbers.

OLEOMARGARINE

- like butter, oleomargarine picks up flavors and aromas from other foods in the refrigerator. So keep it well covered.

- if you like the texture and easy spreadability of whipped oleomargarine, it's very easy to make—and cheap. Let a stick of regular oleomargarine come to room temperature, then whip it to lightness with an electric beater. Add 3 tablespoons of salad oil, 1 at a time, and whip everything up well. With a rubber spatula, transfer the mixture to a small bowl, cover tightly, and refrigerate. This also increases the volume of the original stick of oleomargarine.

■ if you're out of regular oleomargarine and absolutely have to use whipped oleomargarine in baking, weigh it–don't go by volume.

OMELETS: see EGGS

ONIONS
■ see also *Scallions*.
■ 1 small onion, finely chopped, will give you ¼ cup.
■ onions that show a bit of green spear growing out of them should be used at once, otherwise they will spoil.
■ if you have an onion that's begun to sprout, put it in a pot with a drainage hole, fill the pot with soil–the onion should be only about half-covered–water it well, and set the pot in the light. Keep the surface moderately moist. The onion will grow lots of green sprouts. Snip just as you would chives or scallions. The sprouts will continue to grow for weeks (very nice in the wintertime), and you'll always have some nippy greens at hand for soups, salads, and a multitude of other uses.
■ a wet onion is much easier to peel than a dry one.
■ a partially frozen onion is easy to slice and chop and–best of all–causes no tears.
■ onions tend to discolor when cut with a carbon steel (as opposed to stainless steel) knife. This won't matter for onions intended for cooking, but you might prefer to use a stainless knife if you're slicing onion rings for salad, for example.
■ if you need to cut an onion in whole round slices, hang on to the tail end of the onion as you cut. After each slice, turn the onion slightly on the cutting board before you cut the next slice. This will minimize the tendency to cut on the bias.

■ to take the bite out of raw onion slices you intend to serve in salad or for a sandwich, soak the slices for an hour in tepid water that has been sweetened with a little sugar (about 1 teaspoon to a measuring cup of water).

■ if a recipe calls for chopped onion as an ingredient, reduce the amount called for and grate it instead. You get more of an onion flavor and it's easier to distribute.

■ anything you cook with onions will need less liquid than when cooked without. Onions contain a great deal of moisture.

■ if you're adding onions to a stock that will later be strained and the vegetables discarded, don't bother to peel the onions. Just wash them and cut them up. The same is true of garlic. Save yourself work.

■ put slices of onion in a low oven and heat them until golden brown and absolutely dry. Save the slices in a jar to use for stews, soups, and sauces. They'll give a richer taste and a more beautiful color than plain onions.

ORANGES

■ 1 dozen oranges will give you about 4 cups of juice.

■ pale oranges, or even those showing some green, are just as good inside as those that are bright orange in color.

■ oranges, like grapefruit and lemons, should be open to the air during storage. Don't put them in closed bags or the skins will mildew.

■ oranges with very rough surfaces are thick-skinned and generally have less juice and meat inside. But they're preferable if you want orange sections.

■ whole oranges can be peeled quickly and their sections separated cleanly if you cover them with boiling water and let them stand for 5 minutes. Then pour off the water, cool the fruit, and peel.

■ instead of throwing away orange skins, cut into strips and freeze them. The strips are very handy for flavoring all kinds of desserts.

■ orange juice that comes in cartons is of two kinds: plain, refrigerated orange juice; or reconstituted, which means the juice has been dehydrated, mixed with water, and become juice again. The second kind is often somewhat cheaper.

■ if you make orange juice from frozen concentrate, you'll get a tastier glass of juice if you squeeze some fresh orange juice into each glass, then fill the remainder of the glass with the reconstituted juice.

OVENS

■ see also *Baking, Energy Savers.*

■ some basic oven temperature equivalents you should know are:

	Fahrenheit	Celsius (metric)
Low oven	250°	121°
Moderate oven	350°	177°
Hot oven	450°	232°
Broil	550°	288°

■ a gas oven with a pilot light can be a fine dryer for glassware. Put the washed glasses in and leave with just the pilot going. They'll come out crystal clear.

■ you can also dry washed pots and pans in a gas oven with a pilot light.

■ an electric self-cleaning oven can make defrosting your freezer a cinch. Stash all the frozen foods in the oven and keep the door closed. A self-cleaning electric oven is usually so well insulated that it will even keep ice cubes frozen for 2 hours.

With the frozen foods safely packed away, you can defrost your freezer without worrying about them.

- ■ to reduce the heat in your oven quickly for a special purpose, put in a large pan of cold water.

OYSTERS: see SHELLFISH

PANCAKES

- see also *Blender*.
- the rule for light, tender pancakes is the same as for biscuits and muffins: Stir the batter only until the ingredients are evenly mixed, no more.
- for perfectly round pancakes, let the batter pour straight down from the tip of a large spoon. The batter will make a circle all by itself.
- a pancake is ready to be turned when it's puffed and the top surface is evenly covered with small bubbles. With an average batter, this takes about 2 minutes on the first side and 1 minute on the other. Never turn a pancake more than once—this toughens it.
- if your pancake recipe calls for melted butter, be sure the milk and eggs are at room temperature before the butter is added, otherwise it will harden.
- substitute other kinds of flour for half of the white flour called for in your recipe. Use buckwheat flour or fine cornmeal or rice flour, etc. You can make a flour by putting cereals in the blender. You'll have wonderful tasting pancakes, and more healthful ones, too.
- you can substitute vegetable oil for butter or oleomargarine in pancakes, but the cooked pancake is likely to be a little less brown.
- use orange juice or some other fruit juice instead of milk. Add ¼ teaspoon of baking soda to the flour.

■ dip bread slices in leftover pancake batter, then sauté as you would French toast. Marvelous with cinnamon and sugar, jam, preserves, or syrup.

PAPAYA
■ squeeze or rub the juice of a papaya over a tough cut of meat. It contains enzymes that are an excellent meat tenderizer.

PAPRIKA: see HERBS AND SPICES

PARSLEY: see HERBS AND SPICES

PASTA
■ see also *Sauces and Gravies, Storage Tips.*
■ 1 pound of noodles, cooked, will give you about 9 cups.
■ 1 average portion of spaghetti and spaghettini, when served as a main dish, weighs about 140 grams (5 ounces) uncooked, or the amount that, when tightly bunched together and held upright, will cover the surface of a nickel.
■ add 1 teaspoon of salt and 1 tablespoon of oil to every quart of water you cook pasta in.
■ there's a very old joke about how to tell when spaghetti is done: Throw a handful against the wall and if it sticks, it's done. But why ruin the kitchen wall? Wind a strand from the cooking pot onto a fork, then pinch the doubled or tripled strand between your fingers. There should be a slight—but very slight—resistance before you pinch the strand into separate pieces. If it seems hard in the middle, keep the spaghetti cooking a bit longer. But you don't want it mushy, so watch it.
■ what does *al dente* mean? It means firm to the teeth.
■ if you're worried about overcooking spaghetti or other pasta (or if you have to cook it ahead of time), boil it to the

point where it's still somewhat tough, take the pot from the heat, and let it stand quietly, covered. It will slowly absorb more water and become a little softer—never mushy. When you're ready to eat, heat the pasta quickly only until it's hot, then drain and serve.

- don't rinse pasta after you've boiled it. I don't know how such an idea ever got started.

- cooked, well-drained spaghetti can be pressed over the bottom and sides of a pie pan, and filled with any creamed chicken, fish, meat, or vegetable, or with a cheese filling. Bake it. The pasta bakes into a nice crust.

PASTRY: see PIES

PASTRY BAG
- for a quick, no-mess, disposable pastry bag, put icing, etc., in a clean plastic bag, the kind you store food in. Twist the bag closed, snip a tiny piece off a bottom corner and squeeze.

PASTRY BRUSH
- a 1-inch nylon or bristle paintbrush makes a fine pastry brush.

PÂTÉ: see BLENDER, HORS D'OEUVRES, LEFTOVERS

PEACHES
- a pound of peaches, sliced, will give you about 2 cups.
- peaches spoil rapidly if they're bruised. Be sure to handle carefully when packing or storing.
- peaches that are hard and show a lot of green on their skins will never ripen properly. Avoid them.
- peaches will ripen in a brown paper bag if you put an apple in with them. The apple releases a natural gas (ethylene)

that aids in ripening. This is the same gas, by the way, that causes tomatoes to ripen.

- to slow down the ripening of peaches, refrigerate them.
- to make spiced peaches at much less than the cost of buying them, simmer canned whole peaches (or apricots) with cloves and a little real maple syrup and brandy added to the canned juice.

PEANUT BUTTER
- see also *Nuts*.
- peanut butter is a good–and relatively inexpensive–source of protein. It does not have the protein quality found in meat, but it has more than other commonly eaten vegetable products.
- an unopened jar of peanut butter will stay in good condition from 6 months to 1 year. Once opened, it should be refrigerated. It will remain in top condition for 3 months.
- refrigerating peanut butter slows down the possible growth of molds or bacteria, and helps to prevent the oils from becoming rancid.
- to make peanut butter in a blender, grind the nuts as fine as possible and then add a little oil. Home blenders are not as powerful as commercial grinders, but the result is very good indeed. (You can also make other interesting nut butters; see *Nuts*.)
- stir 1 tablespoon of strong hot coffee into 2 tablespoons of crunchy peanut butter. Mix this combination into softened vanilla ice cream and put it in the freezer for an hour or so. This could be what the gods on Mount Olympus ate for dessert.
- for a change in peanut butter sandwiches, try mixing pure unsweetened peanut butter–the natural kind that has no added sugar, salt, or oils–with some honey.
- beat a couple of tablespoons of creamy peanut butter

into a white or golden cake batter, then bake as usual.

■ peanut butter is great in soup! Add it to chicken stock with a little butter-and-flour thickener and some light cream. Add sautéed onions if you like. (This is a famous Southern soup.)

■ peanut butter is a legitimate ingredient in a meat sauce. Mix it with soy sauce, lemon juice, a bit of sugar or honey, a little hot sauce if you like your sauces hot, and just enough boiling water to give it the consistency you want. Good on chicken, too.

■ spread peanut butter on a slice of bread, add slices of bananas, top it with another slice of bread. This is known as a Paradise Sandwich.

■ cucumber slices spread over a layer of peanut butter also make a delicious sandwich.

PEARS
■ firm Bosc pears are good baking pears. Bake just as you do apples.

PEAS
■ 1 pound of dry split peas, cooked, will give you about 5 cups.

■ wash the pods of peas before you shell them. After shelling, throw the pods into your stock or soup pot. Cook for 30 minutes and remove them. They'll add a nice flavor.

■ if you like fresh cooked peas slightly sweet, cook them with a few of the empty pods, then remove the pods before serving.

PECANS: see NUTS

PEPPERS
- red peppers are green peppers that have ripened.
- many green peppers have very little flavor. Try to pick ones that show a little yellow or even some red on them. These peppers are on their way to developing a taste.
- to peel a green pepper (for antipasto, marinated peppers, etc.), wash and dry firm peppers, broil them on a rack about 5 inches from the heat for about 10 minutes, or until the skins begin to wrinkle and brown. Turn them now and then. Let cool, then hold them under cold water. The skin will peel off easily.

PERSIMMONS
- you can remove much of the astringency from a persimmon if you wrap it airtight with an apple for 24 hours.
- an unripe persimmon is full of tannic acid and will give you a long-lasting dose of mouth pucker! So be sure the persimmon is ripe before you bite into it. A ripe persimmon is soft, with a yellow to dark-orange skin color. The flesh itself is bright orange. To ripen persimmons, seal them at room temperature in a plastic bag with a couple of ripe apples. Refrigerate them when they're ripe.
- a ripe persimmon is one fruit that gets sweeter when kept in the cold. So keep them in your refrigerator.
- to purée persimmon pulp for a fruit sauce, add about 1½ teaspoons of lemon juice to each cup of pulp to prevent discoloration.
- put a persimmon in the freezer for about 6 hours. Cut it in half and serve it. It's like a sherbet.

PICKLES
- when you're making pickles of any kind, use whole—

not ground—spices and herbs. Ground spices "muddy" the pickling liquid and also darken the pickles.

■ the leftover juice from sweet pickles is great for soaking dried vegetable flakes (carrots, celery, onions, pepper, etc.). After the flakes have marinated in the juice for a couple of days, use in salads and canapé mixtures.

■ the juice from canned pickles can be mixed with oil and used as a salad dressing. It's also very good for making a sweet-and-sour meat gravy.

PIES
■ see also *Berries, Crumbs and Crumb Crusts, Meringues.*

PASTRY
■ never attempt to mix pastry dough in a hot kitchen. The success of pastry depends on all the ingredients remaining as cold as possible for as long as possible until baked.

■ too much water added to pie pastry will make it tough and more likely to shrink.

■ for a flaky pie pastry, add a teaspoon of vinegar or lemon juice to the water when you mix.

■ ordinary pie pastry tends to become monotonous. Give it some character by adding ingredients to improve the flavor and texture. If the pastry is for a meat or chicken pie, use a little curry powder in the mix, or a tablespoon of sesame seeds. Use any additions—cinnamon, chili powder, ginger—that seem to you to go with the filling.

■ a pie shell made (and refrigerated) the day before it's baked will be crispier after baking.

■ most cookie dough makes dandy pie pastry, especially for open-faced tarts, etc. Knead the dough a little, roll it out thin, and fit it into the pie pan as you would pastry dough.

- pastry for the top and bottom crusts of a 9-inch pie pan should be about 11 inches in diameter.

- when you divide a ball of pastry dough for rolling the top and bottom crusts, put a little more dough into the portion for the top crust. You can press, stretch, and patch the bottom crust once it's in the pan because it's going to be filled, but be sure the top crust is ample enough to cover the pie smoothly.

- to transfer the circle of pastry dough from the rolling surface to the pie pan without stretching or tearing it, flour the rolling pin well and drape the pastry circle loosely over it. Have the pie pan close by so you can lift the dough immediately into it.

- another method of getting a circle of pastry dough neatly into the pie pan—after you've rolled it out—is to roll the dough very lightly into a cylinder, tilt the pan so you can roll the cylinder into it, then unroll the dough.

- after you've placed the bottom crust in the pie pan, the crust is less likely to shrink if you let it stand for about 5 minutes before you fill it or handle it in any way.

- roll leftover pie pastry into strips, give them a light coating of butter, honey, or jam, dust with cinnamon, and bake. Utterly delicious!

CRUSTS
- if you want a pie to have a well-browned bottom crust, bake it in a dark metal pie pan.

- to give a pie a lovely color when baked, melt 1 tablespoon of butter in 2 tablespoons of milk and brush the top of the unbaked pie with this.

- if you want a shiny, brittle crust on a pie, paint the surface of the top crust with a mixture of 1 whole egg beaten with 1 teaspoon of water before you bake the pie.

■ brush the top crust of an unbaked pie with a little milk, dot with 1 tablespoon of shortening, and sprinkle with a mixture of 1 tablespoon of sugar, 3 tablespoons of flour, ½ teaspoon each of cinnamon and grated lemon or orange rind. This will give you a nice crisp, crumbly topping when baked.

■ to get a flaky crust on a pie, spread the crust with ½ teaspoon of soft shortening mixed with 1½ teaspoons of soft butter. Dust the crust with flour and sprinkle with a little water, then bake.

■ to easily remove the wedges of a pie made with graham cracker crust, butter the inside of the pie pan very well before you press the crumbs into it.

■ a graham cracker pie crust is less likely to crumble when you cut it if you hold the pie pan in warm water for 30 seconds, about halfway up the side, just before you're ready to serve.

FILLINGS

■ if a pie filling contains molasses, use a deep-dish pan or even a cake pan to bake the pie in. Molasses usually bubbles high during baking and might run over. To be safer still, set the pan on a cookie sheet.

■ one way to avoid a runny filling and a soggy crust in a custard pie is to be sure that both the cooked pastry shell and the custard are cool before you fill the shell.

■ to see if a baked custard pie is done, insert a knife blade near the edge of the pie (not in the middle). If the knife comes out clean, the custard's done. The middle part of a baked custard pie firms during cooling.

■ for a variation of the traditional lemon custard pie that calls for lemon juice, slice the lemon paper-thin and include the slices with the lemon juice. This makes a marvelous pie. You can also cut the lemon slices into thin strips—this makes cutting the pie wedges a bit easier.

■ a couple of tablespoons of honey added to the pumpkin filling when you're preparing a pumpkin pie will give an attractive shiny glaze on the pie after it's baked.

■ you will need 4 cups of fresh berries to make a 9-inch pie.

■ juices in a berry pie are likely to run under the bottom crust during baking, but you can keep the crust from sticking to the pan if you grease the pie pan and dust it with flour before setting in the bottom crust.

■ if you like to serve cheese with apple pie, try baking the cheese *into* the pie. Spread grated Cheddar over the bottom crust before you add the filling. Or sprinkle the cheese over the top of the pie before the last 15 minutes of baking.

■ pies, especially fruit pies, are more delicious if you stick them in the oven and give them a good warming just before you serve them.

■ to get a glaze on your fruit pies or tarts, brush the surface with heated corn syrup as soon as you've taken them from the oven.

■ the fillings of many pie recipes can be baked as is, without a crust. Many can be cut into wedges and served; others can be treated as hot puddings, served with a spoon, and topped with anything that seems appropriate to you.

PIMIENTOS
■ the unused portion of a can or jar of pimientos will last longer, without spoiling, if you drain the pimientos well and cover them with salad oil. Store in the refrigerator.

PINEAPPLE
- 1 pineapple, cubed, will give you about 2½ cups.
- if a pineapple hasn't ripened on the tree, it never will. It may get softer, but it won't get sweeter. Test for ripeness by pulling out one of the center top leaves. The leaf will come out easily if the fruit is ripe. Also, a ripe pineapple will smell sweet and fruity, and the sharp outer coat will have lost all green color.
- if one side of a pineapple is very much lighter in color than the rest of the rind, avoid it—it will be dry inside.
- to get fancy pineapple strips for a special fruit dessert, cut the fresh pineapple into spears and put them in a jar. Cover the spears with raspberry juice (this can be the juice from frozen raspberries) and let them stand in the refrigerator for 24 hours. They'll be a beautiful color, and taste gorgeous.
- wash the knife thoroughly after you've cut the rind from a pineapple and before you slice it. Pineapple rind contains a mouth irritant that causes a burning sensation in some people—and a residue of the irritant may cling to the knife.

PLUMS
- if fresh plums are brownish on one side, they're likely to have a poor flavor.

POMEGRANATES
- cut a pomegranate in half and juice it like an orange—it's divine.

POTATOES
- see also *Sweet Potatoes and Yams.*
- potatoes that are partly green, or have green spots on them, are often bitter.
- some potatoes have a hollow, darkish center when you

cut them open. (There's no way to tell from the outside.) Such a condition is more likely to occur in very large, mature potatoes.

■ potatoes stored in the refrigerator become somewhat sweeter than potatoes kept in a warmer place or at room temperature.

■ to freeze raw, unpeeled potatoes, wrap them individually, airtight. When you need them, let them defrost at room temperature, then peel. (They peel easily.) They're fine for boiling and mashing.

■ potatoes with a good starch content (mealy ones) are best for boiling and baking. To test whether the potatoes are of the proper variety, cut one in half crosswise and rub the two halves against each other briskly. If the potato has plenty of starch, it will produce a frothy juice as you rub it.

■ potatoes eaten with their skins on have more nutrients than other starches traditionally served with a meal: white bread, rice, noodles. The only exception is dried beans, which are right up there with potatoes. But potatoes eaten without their skins are at about the same level as the other three starches.

■ if you're going to eat potatoes with their skins, scrub the potatoes very well before cooking. Many potatoes are sprayed with a chemical to keep the "eyes" from sprouting. This chemical is soluble in water. (To be safest, scrub potatoes with a brush and soapy water, and rinse well.)

■ potatoes cooked whole lose fewer nutrients than those cut up.

■ potatoes cooked with their skins on are very easy to peel while hot.

■ when baking or boiling potatoes, choose those that are as close to the same size as possible. They'll all be cooked to the same degree at the same time.

BAKED

■ long and slow baking will give you a drier, mealier potato, regardless of the kind of potato.

■ you can shorten the baking time of a potato if you remove a very thick slice from each end (after you've scrubbed it well) and oil the cut ends slightly before setting the potato in the oven.

■ if you like the skin of your baked potato tender instead of crusty, pour a little oil in your palms and rub it on the potato before baking. Or wrap the potato in aluminum foil before baking; this, however, will give it a steamed rather than baked flavor.

■ if you like a sour cream topping on your baked potato but would like to ease up on the fats and calories, use cottage cheese. Put it in the blender and whip to smoothness. If you want to thin the cottage cheese, whip in a tiny bit of milk. Add garlic or onion and some pepper, if you like.

■ another great topping for a baked potato that steers clear of sour cream is yogurt mixed with chopped chives or finely minced fresh mint.

■ to freeze baked stuffed potatoes, wrap them individually in aluminum foil. Put them, still wrapped and frozen, in a moderate oven for about 25 minutes just before you're ready to eat them. Open and test to see if they're thawed and hot—they may need 5 or so minutes more.

BOILED

■ when you boil potatoes (to serve boiled, or for potato salad), add some pepper, onion, and a bay leaf to the cooking water. Or drop in a chicken bouillon cube. Any of these will greatly improve the flavor.

■ boiled potatoes always become soggy if you put them

in a covered dish. You can, however, keep them warm by putting them in a dish and covering them with a napkin.

■ because some potatoes contain less moisture than others, you may find it necessary when mashing boiled potatoes to add a fair amount of liquid—milk, cream, or some of the potato water—to bring them to proper fluffiness.

■ when you boil potatoes for mashing, mix some of the hot potato water with powdered milk and a little butter or oil. Add this to the hot potatoes as you mash for a more flavorful and nutritious dish.

MASHED

■ if you beat some heavy cream, whipped and lightly salted, into mashed potatoes, they become absolutely heavenly.

■ to mash potatoes that have become waterlogged from overcooking, drain them well, beat with an electric beater, adding dry skimmed milk powder as you beat. Use as much powder as is necessary to make a bowl of light, airy potatoes.

■ the best mashed potatoes in the world are made from *baked* potatoes. Bake them as you usually do, scoop out the lovely steaming interior, add some hot milk or cream and possibly some butter as you beat. (Don't throw away those crispy skins—eat them while you work in the kitchen.)

SAUTÉING AND FRYING

■ don't sauté too many potato pieces at one time. They tend to steam and stick together.

■ to make hashed brown potatoes brown quickly, wash, peel, dry, and slice the potatoes. Then dredge them lightly in a bowl of flour. Shake off the flour, put the slices into hot fat in a skillet, and sauté as usual.

■ while you're pan-frying potatoes, sauté in another pan

some well-drained sauerkraut until it's very lightly browned. Add the sauerkraut to the fried potatoes with a little pepper. Mix well, heat some more, and serve. Wonderful!

■ a potato cutter used for making french fries can be used to make diced potatoes, too. Slice the potatoes first, as for french fries, then cut the potato sticks at right angles into cubes so the dice will be uniform in size.

POT HOLDERS

■ pot holders thick enough to really protect your hands from the extreme heat of very hot pot handles are hard to find. If you know how to knit, you can make great pot holders out of odds and ends of yarn. The trick is to use a fairly thin needle and to purl both sides. This will give you thick, usable pot holders.

■ don't grab a towel to use in place of a pot holder. The ends may catch fire.

POT ROASTS: see PRESSURE COOKER

POTS AND PANS

■ see also *Pressure Cooker.*

■ generally speaking, the thicker the metal of a pot, the more even is the distribution of heat.

■ before you buy any pan, pick it up to check the weight. Check, especially, to see if the handle is comfortable for you.

■ if you use an electric range, be sure your pots and pans have absolutely flat bottoms. This ensures that no heat is lost between the burner and the pot.

■ to season a cast-iron pot, rub the inside generously with cooking oil (use a paper towel). Then set the pot in a low to moderate oven (300° to 325° F) for an hour. Turn the heat off and let the pot stand for several hours or overnight. Remove it and wipe it well. It will stay in tip-top condition if you give the inside a wipe with a little oil every now and then, after you've washed it.

■ use a permanent marker to label the outsides of pots, casseroles, etc., whose capacity you can't always remember. You will save a lot of time when you need to know if a particular pot or casserole has the capacity the recipe calls for.

■ cake, pie, and bread pans do a better job of baking when they're not shining and gleaming, so don't knock yourself out to scrub all the baking stains off them.

■ if you need a cover for a pie plate or a low baking dish and your pot lids don't fit, try inverting a pot or skillet over the top.

■ foods cook more quickly in a covered pan. Water also comes to a boil faster if the pot or kettle has a cover.

■ it's almost instinct to rap a spoon or fork against the edge of a pot to dislodge food you've been stirring. But be warned: If the pot is enamel covered, it will eventually crack and splinter.

■ salt and a little lemon juice will usually remove burned stains from the outside of enamel pots.

■ if your stove is electric, try to match the size of the pot to the size of the burner when you cook.

■ cool a hot pot down a little before you pour very cold water on it. The reaction may not be as dramatic as with glass, but metals can be damaged by sudden profound changes in temperature.

■ if the tin lining of a copper pan begins to wear through, you must have it relined. Acid foods cooked on a copper surface can be harmful when eaten.

■ if the inside of an aluminum pan darkens, heat a little vinegar and water in it. Or cook something that is high in acid, and the discoloration will disappear.

- for some top-of-stove cooking, use a slightly larger pot than usual for mixtures that require stirring. The contents will be less likely to overflow during boiling. And for soups and stews, the stirring can be more thorough.

- always lift the cover of a cooking pot with the opening turned away from you so you won't get a burst of steam in your face.

- to line casseroles or pots and pans that are going into the oven, turn them over and fit aluminum foil over the bottom. Turn the top side up and place the formed piece of foil inside. It will fit in quite neatly.

- always rinse out a pan before you pour any liquid into it for heating. This will keep the liquid (milk or broth, for instance) from scorching the sides of the pan as it heats.

- you'll have an easy time cleaning casseroles and pans if you simply fill them with cold water and let them soak overnight.

- you can eliminate most of the burned flavor caused by scorching if you immediately set the scorched pan in a little cool water or on a cold wet towel before you turn the contents (without scraping) into another pan.

- turn a cooking pot now and then, whether it's on a burner or in the oven, to equalize the heat. Many people don't think of this, but if you use this technique, it is less likely that the bottom of a pot will overheat in any one spot.

PRESSURE COOKER

- among the many wonderful uses of a pressure cooker is cooking a beef heart. Inexpensive, as beef goes, and when cooked to tenderness—which a pressure cooker does very well—a beef heart has as much flavor as a pot roast. Delicious!

- pressure cookers were made for pot roasts. The toughest meat comes out tender, sweet, and juicy. Although the less expensive cuts of meat are generally tougher, the tougher meats actually have more flavor. And with a pressure cooker the problem of toughness is taken care of. So pressure-cook inexpensive cuts and you'll save money and time.

■ the same holds true for fowl. Tough old hens and roosters are a lot less expensive per pound than younger ones. If you know how to use pressure-cooking methods, you can make a marvelous dish of chicken stew to feed a large family for relatively little cost.

■ pressure cookers are ideal for making good old-fashioned steamed puddings—plum, mincemeat, apple, molasses puddings, etc.

■ if you are a jelly maker, you ought to know that cooking fruit in a pressure cooker extracts a quarter more of the juice than top-of-stove cooking does.

■ rice cooks in about 8 minutes in a pressure cooker. If you're cooking it for rice pudding, increase the cooking time by a couple of minutes so the rice will come out soft and creamy, the way it *should* be for a pudding.

■ the pressure cooker is great for making soup stocks. If there's one thing that usually needs a lot of time to cook in order to develop flavor, it's stock. But why cook bones and meat and vegetable scraps for hours on top of the stove to extract all their goodness when you can accomplish the same thing in an hour with a pressure cooker?

PRUNES
■ to stuff prunes, soften them first by pouring boiling water over them and let stand away from the heat until the water cools. Drain, pit, and stuff.

PUDDINGS
■ see also *Pressure Cooker.*

■ to keep a skin from forming on top of a boiled pudding made with cornstarch, which includes butterscotch, chocolate, or vanilla puddings, set a piece of waxed paper flat against the surface of the pudding before you chill it.

■ a baked rice pudding will be softer and creamier if you set the baking dish in a pan holding about an inch of hot water. Then bake.

■ when you're cooling a boiled rice pudding, stir it now and then to prevent the rice from sinking to the bottom.

■ use inexpensive short-grain rice to make a baked or boiled rice pudding. The rice will absorb the milk more quickly if you cook the rice first in rapidly boiling water for 5 minutes, then drain. Proceed with the pudding as usual.

■ a bread pudding will taste much better if you serve it warm with a little warmed maple syrup poured over it. Or try it with a caramel sauce.

■ substitute chocolate chips or chopped dates for raisins in bread pudding.

PUMPKINS: see SQUASH AND PUMPKINS

QUICHE

- you don't have to make a traditional pastry crust for a quiche. Instead, remove the crusts from very thin slices of white bread and press the bread firmly into a well-buttered pie or quiche pan. Fill in any cracks with soft bread crumbs. Cover with your quiche filling and bake.

RAISINS

- a 15-ounce box of raisins equals 2½ cups.
- raisins, as an ingredient in cakes or puddings, will usually benefit by plumping first: Pour a warmed liquid over them and simmer for about 5 minutes. The liquid can be water, wine, any liquor, or fruit juice. Drain, and use the raisin liquid, if possible, in place of an equal amount of liquid called for in the recipe.
- raisins are easier to chop if you freeze them first.
- if raisins in an opened box are beginning to dry out, pour them into a jar and cover them with any fruit-flavored brandy or liqueur. They'll keep indefinitely and are wonderful to use in desserts or dessert sauces. Drained well, they'll give a lift to your homemade raisin bread, too.

RASPBERRIES: see BERRIES

REHEATING

- when you're cooking a meat or vegetable dish that you intend to reheat before serving, remember it should be slightly underdone at the end of the first cooking.

RHUBARB

- 1 pound of diced rhubarb will give you about 3½ cups; 1 pound cooked, 2 cups.

- to make a 9-inch pie, you will need 6 cups of diced rhubarb.
- the young, early season rhubarb is the best to use when making pie. The more mature stalks are inclined to be tough and stringy in a pie. Use them for stewing.

RICE
- see also *Puddings.*
- if kept well wrapped or in tightly closed jars, white rice can be stored safely for a couple of years.
- if you want to substitute converted rice for regular raw white rice, use ⅔ cup of the converted for each ½ cup of the regular.
- brown rice takes somewhat longer to cook and absorbs more water than white rice, although the cooking method is the same. Allow an extra 10 to 15 minutes if you're substituting brown for white.
- stirring rice while it's cooking makes it pasty and gummy.
- any rice dish (not just rice pudding) will have a greatly enhanced flavor if you add a little cinnamon at the beginning of cooking.
- a way to test rice to see if it's done is to press a grain between your thumb and forefinger—you should feel no hard center.
- rice cooks in about 8 minutes in a pressure cooker. If you're cooking it for rice pudding, increase the cooking time by a couple of minutes and the rice will come out soft and creamy, the way it *should* be for rice pudding.
- water left over from cooking rice is good to use when making gravy. The gravy will need less thickening.

RUBBER HOUSEHOLD GLOVES

■ rubber gloves for use in the kitchen should be as long as possible—halfway up to the elbow, at least. No wet wrists.

■ always dust the inside of rubber gloves with talcum powder before putting them on. If you don't, each time you remove them you'll stretch the rubber. And in time tiny, invisible holes will let the water in.

■ cut a large square or round patch from a worn-out rubber glove to drape over the lid of a hard-to-open jar. It will give you a good grip.

SALAD DRESSINGS

- see also *Blender*.
- the secret of a fine salad dressing—one that isn't unduly sharp—lies in the vinegar. Don't use distilled or cider vinegar. Even many of the red wine vinegars are a bit too caustic. Look for rice wine vinegar, a soft white vinegar that's just right for most cooking uses. You'll find it in Chinese or Japanese food sections of some supermarkets.
- it's not always necessary to mix a dressing before you pour it on the salad. Be sure the greens are well drained and on the dry side, then pour on olive oil or salad oil and toss to coat the leaves. Pour off any excess. Then add a little vinegar (flavored or unflavored) or lemon juice. Most salads need little else.
- make an interesting low-calorie salad dressing by using tomato juice in place of the oil and vinegar. Add herbs of your choice, a little garlic or onion, and pepper. Mix in the blender.
- a cooked salad dressing is less likely to curdle if you chill the vinegar and stir the beaten eggs into it before you put the pan on the heat. (It's best to make a cooked dressing in a double boiler, over hot water.)
- grate a little fresh ginger root into a salad dressing and shake well.
- use the juice from a jar of pickles (plus oil) to make a really tasty salad dressing.

■ the oil from canned fish, mixed with lemon juice and a little pepper, makes a wonderful salad dressing.

■ for a slightly out-of-the-ordinary salad dressing, try any of these: sour cream or yogurt mixtures; sweet and sour dressing (tomato and brown sugar); mustard sauce; horseradish sauce; soy sauce.

■ add a small piece of boiled potato, very well mashed, to salad dressing. It helps to form an emulsion that holds the ingredients together.

■ you can use practically any salad dressing as a marinade for such foods as ripe olives, mushrooms, and most vegetables (if you blanch them first)—cauliflowerets, green or red sweet peppers, small onions, green beans, etc. Marinate in the dressing for a day or so in the refrigerator.

■ to make delicious hamburger, mix leftover salad dressing in it. Leftover salad dressing is also good mixed with flaked fish or chopped hard-cooked eggs for sandwiches.

SALADS

■ see also *Lettuce.*

■ salad greens keep better when dry and cool. So don't wash them before you store them in the refrigerator unless you intend to use them within 24 hours.

■ many wilted greens can be brought back to life if you soak them for a short time in very cold water, remove any brown parts, roll the greens in a dish towel, and stow in the refrigerator.

■ serve a salad with your dinner every day. It's a great meal extender and marvelous as a method of using leftovers. One head of lettuce, properly prepared, can last for several meals. Remove 4 or 5 leaves each day, wash, dry, and tear them up. Add bits of anything else you have: cut-up celery, raw or cooked vegetables, perhaps a piece of tomato, some minced onion. A little goes a long way in a salad and the cost is low.

▪ you can serve practically any salad green as a hot vegetable. Prepare as you would spinach and sauté or braise. Lettuce can usually stand a little extra flavoring such as celery seed, pepper, a little garlic, etc.

▪ pare broccoli stems, and slice the crisp interiors to use as a salad vegetable.

▪ very young dandelion greens, those found growing in early spring, are lovely when added raw to a leafy salad.

▪ who says you must have lettuce in every salad? You can make wonderful salads with no greens at all. Some possibilities to serve alone with a dressing—or two or three combined with either a dressing or plain lemon or lime juice—are: sliced tomatoes sprinkled with any kind of fresh herbs; drained and rinsed sauerkraut; grated raw turnip; orange sections; celery cut in crosswise slices; sliced onions, tamed by soaking in sweetened water; carrot slices, lightly poached, then chilled.

▪ if you dress a salad before serving it, don't serve it in the same bowl in which you've mixed it. After the mixing, transfer the salad, using tongs or double forks, to the serving bowl. This ensures that the salad will not sit in a pool of dressing. There should be only enough dressing in the serving bowl to coat the pieces.

▪ before adding an egg to a Caesar salad, cook it in boiling water for 1 minute. Then break it over the salad greens and add the flavored salad oil. Add the bread cubes last. Toss well with two spoons.

▪ heat finely shredded leftover salad in consommé, bouillon, or any stock you have on hand. This makes a lovely soup.

▪ if you're out of croutons to strew over a tossed salad, use dry cereals such as Rice Chex, Wheat Chex, shredded wheat bits, etc.

SALT

■ there's no need to add salt to the water in which you cook vegetables. In fact, salt toughens many vegetables in the cooking–this is particularly true of beans.

■ it probably wouldn't hurt many of us to cut down on the amount of salt we take in daily. We ought to stop deadening our tongues to the taste of salt by overusing it. You'll be surprised how you can taste the natural salt in most foods. Beef, for example, is naturally high in salt. If you get used to preparing it with very little–or no–salt, you'll discover that a beef roast can be adequately salty in its natural state.

■ natural peanut butter–ground to order with nothing but roasted peanuts–is a godsend for people on low-salt diets. (You can sometimes buy this in grocery stores–check the labels.)

■ if you're on a low-salt diet, use–as your imagination directs–powdered mustard, powdered onion, almost all spices, lemon juice or lemon wedges, sugar, honey, vanilla and other flavoring extracts, diced fruits, and berries.

■ to cut down on salt, flavor your food with lemon juice and garlic or a combination of both. Lots of garlic not only makes many a dish taste better, but it's also rich in vitamin C. (And holds vampires at bay!)

■ for low-salt diets, cook chicken, meat, or fish with liberal amounts of paprika. You won't miss the salt.

■ add a little sugar or some honey or an onion to the cooking water for vegetables. It won't occur to you that the salt is missing.

■ if you find you've put too much salt in soup, add a teaspoon each of vinegar and granulated sugar. Or add a teaspoon of brown sugar or molasses. Bring the pot to a simmer.

■ a tablespoon of salt added to a quart of water is sufficient to keep certain fruits and vegetables (peaches, pears, apples, potatoes, avocados, etc.) from discoloring after you've peeled them.

■ a strong solution of salt water will remove fishy odors from a pot.

SANDWICHES

■ see also *Peanut Butter.*

■ if a sandwich filling is loose or very moist, be sure to first spread the bread with a thin layer of cream cheese or butter or oleomargarine.

■ make a basic sandwich spread with 1 part butter and 2 parts cream cheese. To this you can add anything that tastes good to you.

■ there's no reason that vegetables or meats must monopolize sandwich fillings. Consider using fruits. They're great chopped and mixed with cream cheese or cottage cheese, or chopped fine and combined with mayonnaise. (Fruits are good with lots of other cheeses, too.)

■ use two different kinds of bread when you make a sandwich: one slice of white and one of whole wheat, for instance. And you don't have to rely on ordinary bread. Use slices of banana bread or other fruit bread, nut bread, cheese bread, etc. They taste good, and they're nutritious.

■ slice white bread very thin, remove the crusts, butter the *outsides* of two slices, put a layer of finely ground sandwich filling between the slices, and brown in the waffle iron. This is a treat to the eye and to the taste.

■ sandwiches made with cream cheese don't store well, even when wrapped and refrigerated. The cheese tends to dry out and yellow. Eat such sandwiches the same day they're made.

■ put ketchup, mayonnaise, or mustard between the slices of meats, cheese, etc., instead of on the bread. This eliminates sogginess, especially if you make the sandwiches ahead of time.

■ put leftovers in the blender with a little mayonnaise and jazz up the mixture with some seasoning. In no time—a sandwich spread.

SAUCES AND GRAVIES

■ when you're stirring a sauce on the stove, remove the pan from the heat frequently and stir to ensure that the sauce doesn't begin to scorch.

■ to keep a skin from forming on a sauce containing flour, mashed potato, or other starch, top the surface of the sauce with a little cream or melted butter before you refrigerate it. When you're ready to serve, stir well and heat.

■ when you remove a sauce containing eggs from the heat, stir rapidly to cool it. Sauce continues to cook when first taken from the heat and you don't want the inner part of the sauce to heat to the point where the yolks may curdle.

■ when cooking a sauce containing egg yolks in a double boiler, keep the water in the bottom pot at no more than a simmer. If you let the sauce become too hot because of the temperature of the water, the eggs will separate from the rest of the sauce. Play it safe, and lift the top pot out of the water every 10 seconds or so, whisking well as you do this.

■ pour leftover sauce or gravy into a container and freeze it. You can always serve it over something else another day. And if you wish, you can add something new to change its character entirely.

■ break up a few ginger snaps and add enough hot meat gravy to dissolve the pieces thoroughly. Add to the rest of the gravy, stir well, heat, and serve. You have a rich, pungent sauce for any meat dish.

■ keep some chicken or meat broth in your freezer. When you cook chicken or meat requiring a sauce made from their cooking juices, heat the frozen broth to make the sauce, and it will be ready at the same time the chicken or meat is. This does away with the necessity of having to keep the chicken or meat hot while you make the sauce. And the juices from the chicken or meat you've just cooked can be poured into a container and stored in the freezer for use the next time.

■ leftover sauce or gravy from any dish is a good base for spaghetti sauce. In fact, you can make a sauce for any kind of pasta out of almost anything edible. Honest. All that's required is that it have a good flavor and be moderately thick. This should be a challenge—and a great economy—for the imaginative cook.

■ a test for thickness when you're making your own sauce for pasta is to dip a spoon in the cooking sauce; if it coats the spoon, the sauce is thick enough.

■ most spaghetti and other pasta sauces are delicious served over hot cooked vegetables such as broccoli, green beans, and asparagus.

■ pesto sauce is an uncooked—heated—spaghetti (or other pasta) sauce made principally from fresh basil, olive oil, grated cheese, and crushed nuts (pignoli, walnuts, or hazelnuts). You can make this during the fresh basil season. The oil will rise to the top and the sauce will stay very well in the refrigerator for weeks. There should be about ¾ inch of oil on top. For longer storage, freeze small quantities of pesto sauce. It keeps excellently, and you can enjoy it all winter. Use pesto on everything: vegetables, potatoes, fish, and poultry. (Incidentally, if you're making the pesto sauce to freeze, omit the grated cheese. Mix this in after the sauce has thawed.)

■ recipes for chicken, fish, meat, or vegetable sauces can be doubled or even tripled. Refrigerate or freeze whatever's left to serve another day. Many sauces can be served not only hot but cold: for aspics and salads.

■ if you have to carry a container of hot liquid (coffee, tea, gravy, sauce, etc.) for a little distance, stick a spoon in it and it will be less likely to slurp over the rim of the container.

WHITE SAUCE

■ there's nothing like a blender for making white sauce swiftly and easily. Pour all the ingredients into the blender, and mix thoroughly, then pour the mixture into a rinsed pan and heat slowly, stirring with a whisk until the sauce is thickened. No worry about lumps, melting butter, stirring the flour in, etc. It works like magic and gives you a velvety sauce.

■ white sauce lends itself to a great variety of preparations. Here are some possibilities:

■ use part bacon fat or rendered chicken fat for some of the butter called for. Or use some oil.

■ substitute a cup of rich meat stock for an equal amount of milk.

■ use white wine in place of part of the milk.

■ after you've made the sauce, mix in ½ cup of finely grated cheese of any kind.

■ add finely chopped parsley and the cooked white of an egg, finely minced. Sprinkle the hard-cooked yolk over the surface when you serve it.

■ make a caper sauce by adding ½ cup of mayonnaise to your basic sauce and half of a small bottle of drained capers. Heat lightly, don't boil. Great with fish.

■ to make white sauce into brown sauce, heat the flour in a dry pan over medium heat, mixing constantly until it's browned. And use some dark meat stock as part of the liquid.

- use a rich brown stock—instead of milk—and add some curry powder. Now you have a curry sauce.
- substitute ½ cup of white wine for ½ cup of milk, and add a teaspoon or more of prepared mustard.
- if a white sauce is to go over a fish dish, use some fish stock or clam juice as part of your liquid.
- to make a white sauce more delicate, substitute 1 egg yolk for 1 tablespoon of flour (or 2 yolks for 2 tablespoons of flour). But once you add yolks, remember not to boil the sauce—keep it at a low simmer, stirring until it thickens.

SAUERKRAUT

- most canned sauerkraut is too sour for cooking. It should be drained and soaked in cold water for about 10 minutes. After rinsing, soak in white wine. This is great.

SAUTÉING

- sautéing is cooking food in a low-sided pan on top of the stove, using as little fat as possible. You don't, for example, fry eggs—you sauté them. And when you talk about fried potatoes and mean "home fries," you are really referring to sautéed potatoes. (French-fried potatoes are "fried.")
- when you sauté, use the smallest pan the food will fit in. You'll use less fat, and the food will cook more quickly.
- lightly heat a sautéing pan before adding the oil or solid shortening. Once added, continue heating until the oil or shortening begins to bubble. This will do away with the possibility of the food sticking to the pan. (You must be sure the oil or shortening is hot—not smoking—before you add the food.)
- another reason for not putting food in fat until it has reached the bubbling point is that food placed in tepid or cool fat absorbs a great deal of it while cooking.

■ food to be sautéed should be at room temperature. If it is cold, the heat of the hot fat will become temporarily lowered and the food will not only absorb more fat, but also the contrast in temperature will cause the moisture in the food to condense quickly on the surface and make the food stick to the pan.

■ if food to be sautéed is wet, pat it thoroughly dry first; otherwise it will become partially steamed—and you may also get painful spattering.

■ the same is true if you're dipping food into batter, crumbs, or flour before sautéing. It won't cook to crispness unless you pat it dry before you dip it. (It can be downright soggy.)

■ while you're sautéing, shake the pan often so the contents move a little. Do this until the food develops a protective coating that will keep it from sticking to the pan.

■ if you have more food to sauté than one pan will hold, use two pans side by side. In this way everything will be done at the same time.

■ some sautéed food can stay in a hot oven for a short time to be kept warm. But it's never as crisp as when you first lift it from the pan.

SCALLIONS
■ to keep scallions garden fresh for more than a week, stand them—bulb side down—in a glass or jar of cold water. Change the water daily.

SCALLOPS: see SHELLFISH

SHALLOTS
■ shallots, like garlic and onions, are easy to peel if you

wet them first. If you're peeling a lot of them, stand them in hot water for about 10 minutes.

SHELLFISH

- 1 dozen shucked oysters, with their liquid, equal about 1 cup.
- 1 pound of scallops equals about 2 cups.
- hard-shell clams, oysters, scallops—any bivalves you want to open raw—are a cinch to open if first placed in the freezer for 45 minutes to an hour.
- when you make a seafood chowder, add a tablespoon or more of soy sauce, and maybe ¼ cup of sherry to the regular recipe. Simmer another 20 minutes.
- a chicken lobster is a 1-pound lobster.
- a stuffed, broiled live lobster can get very dry during cooking. To preserve moistness, cover the stuffing with large lettuce leaves, then cook the lobster 8 to 10 inches from the broiler for about 25 minutes. Remove the lettuce leaves. If the stuffing needs more browning, let it remain under the broiler for another minute or two. (Use lettuce leaves for the same purpose when you bake a stuffed lobster.)
- a lobster plunged into several quarts of boiling water should cook no longer than 15 minutes, usually. By this time the intestinal vein will have turned bright red—this means the lobster is done.
- lobsters can be steamed as well as boiled. In fact, they'll lose less juice and flavor if you put them, live, in about 3 inches of briskly boiling salted water. Cover at once. Allow 18 to 20 minutes from the time the water boils again. Save the liquid to use as a marvelous soup or fish stock base. Boil it down a bit and freeze it.
- to make lobster stew, let the butter and lobster meat

cool somewhat before you very slowly add the milk. Then put the pot on low heat and stir constantly until the mixture turns a rich salmon color.

■ the secret for the finest lobster stew is to let the cooked dish stand a minimum of 5 hours (in the refrigerator, of course) before reheating and serving. Some Maine lobster catchers maintain that stew is at its best the day after it's made.

■ to stuff a shrimp (the larger size is best for this), shell it, remove the intestinal vein down the back, then slit lengthwise about halfway through along the vein side. Stuff with any mixture you like. Shrimp prepared in this way are best baked.

SHERBET: see ICES

SHORTENING: see FATS AND OILS

SOUFFLÉ
■ you'll have better luck with a soufflé if you spoon the batter, instead of pouring it, from the mixing bowl into the baking dish. Be sure the dish has straight sides.

■ a soufflé will rise higher in the baking dish if you don't grease the side of the pan. (But do grease the bottom.)

■ if you're doubling a soufflé recipe, cook in separate baking dishes. A soufflé won't rise properly if the baking dish is too wide.

SOUPS AND STOCKS
■ see also *Blender, Garnishes, Thickeners.*

SOUPS
■ there's an enormous diversity of what you can put into soup, including leftover meats and vegetables. No matter how

forlorn leftovers look in those little dishes on your refrigerator shelf, they're deliriously happy in the soup pot.

■ the wider the pot you cook soup or stock in, the faster the cooking liquid will evaporate. A heavy, deep, narrow pot with a heavy cover is best. If you use a wide pot, remember to check the water level now and then during cooking.

■ mix a little flour with a little cold water to form a thin, smooth paste, then mix it into puréed soup. It will act as a binder and will keep the puréed vegetables from separating when the soup is standing.

■ don't discard tough broccoli stems or the tougher parts of asparagus or hearts of cabbage. Cook them and purée in the blender. They can be a flavorful and nutritious basis for cream soup.

■ a little honey in tomato-based soup counteracts the acidity and improves the flavor.

■ chop uncooked vegetables (onions, carrots, celery, garlic, green or red peppers, mushrooms, etc.), let them dry out thoroughly, then pulverize them in the blender. Bottle for use in soups and gravies. Or simmer them in water or stock for 10 minutes for a delicious, and practically instant, soup.

■ add a tablespoon or more of soy sauce, and perhaps ¼ cup of sherry, to fish or seafood chowders containing tomatoes. Simmer 10 minutes before serving.

■ you can thicken soup by simmering peeled potatoes in it until they're soft. Then mash them in the liquid. Use a fork or potato masher, or dump the potatoes in the blender with some of the soup.

■ any cooked puréed vegetable will thicken soup. Even cooked onion, when puréed, will thicken soup somewhat.

■ another way to thicken soup is to add ¾ cup of finely grated raw potato to every quart of soup. Simmer for 15 minutes after you've added the potato.

■ still another method of thickening soup is to pour some soup liquid into the blender, add a couple of tablespoons of flour and a teaspoon of butter or oil. Blend until everything is well mixed. Pour back into the soup pot and heat slowly, stirring, until the soup thickens. You can use cornstarch instead of flour to get a translucent soup, much in the style of Chinese soups.

■ some cooks have a prejudice against using flour or cornstarch as a soup thickener. This is unreasonable. Starch is starch, whether its source is wheat, potato, rice, corn, or beans. The important thing is to *cook* the starch. Properly cooked, it need never taste floury. Only raw flour or cornstarch will.

■ rice, lentils, beans, or peas of any variety will thicken soup. Yellow split peas are especially good for this. They'll cook to a nice porridge consistency if you simmer them, covered, in liquid for an hour or so (much less if you soak them overnight first). You don't need to put them in the blender unless you want ultrasmooth soup.

■ noodles, macaroni, and spaghetti broken into bits are marvelous soup thickeners.

■ the final step in soup-making has to do with seasonings. Use the following in various combinations (your choice will depend on the overall nature of the soup): salt, pepper, Worcestershire or Tabasco sauce, minced or powdered garlic, curry powder, chili powder, fresh or dried herbs, a hint of nutmeg, a bit of powdered mustard, a little tomato paste, ½ cup of wine, leftover gravy – the list is endless.

■ if soup is sticking to the bottom of the pot while it's cooking, immediately remove the pot from the heat and let it cool. Only then stir with a wooden spoon, dislodging what's stuck at the bottom and mix well. Don't do this while the pot is hot because the solids won't come free. This hint isn't for soup that has *burned*. If, however, it has burned, pour the soup out of the pot into another pot without disturbing the burned portion at the bottom. You don't want burned solids in your soup.

■ if you have a soup pot going, use it as an adjunct to your other cooking. Instead of cooking whole carrots or potatoes in water to serve as a vegetable, toss them into the soup pot and simmer until done. Remove with a slotted spoon, season, and serve. They'll be a lot more flavorful than if you cooked them in water, and the soup pot will be enriched.

■ here's a way to use up the tail end of a pot of soup and at the same time make a new soup: Purée the last of the soup in the blender, add a little fresh or evaporated milk, spice it up a bit—nutmeg is good—heat, and serve.

STOCKS

■ the liquid part of soup gives the fundamental goodness to the finished dish. Once you've got a thick and fragrant liquid, you can add almost anything to make first-class soup.

■ when you're using bones, chicken, or meat for soup stock, cut the pieces fairly small and cook them in cold water with a little salt added. This pulls out the flavor into the stock.

■ never throw out the juices in which you cook vegetables (or the juices from canned vegetables, either). Save them in a closed jar in the refrigerator, or freeze them. Use for cooking vegetables. Soon this liquid will be so full-flavored that you can use it as the base of a soup.

■ it's not necessary to peel the vegetables that go into soup stock. Scrub well with a brush and water, then cut them up into the stock pot. (Vegetables with a wax coating are not generally used in stock, but if you use them, peel first.)

■ a namby-pamby stock will never make a decent soup. Stock is rarely too rich. If it is, all you have to do is dilute it.

■ don't put too much water in your stock pot. You have

to cook it too long to get rid of the excess liquid. If you think you have too much water, cook the stock without a cover so the excess water will evaporate and the flavors will be more concentrated.

- to flavor stock of any kind, use a little wine or a bit of honey.

- when serving a cold soup, especially a jellied one, chill the cups you're going to serve it in. The soup will remain cold longer and the gelatin won't begin to liquefy.

- if you use canned chicken broth or beef broth as stock for soups or gravies, refrigerate the cans for a day before you open them. The fats will congeal and can be removed by pouring the broth through a fine strainer.

- to make most stocks, cover the bones, meat, or chicken with liquid to a height of 1 inch above the surface of the solids.

- you can make stock in a pressure cooker in about a third of the time it takes to cook it in a regular pot. Be sure *not* to fill the pot higher than the cooker directions tell you.

SOUR CREAM
- see also *Cream*.
- to use yogurt to make your own sour cream—without the fillers so often found in commercial sour cream—mix a heaping tablespoon of yogurt into ½ pint of pure heavy cream (not "ultrapasteurized"—this contains fillers). Be sure the yogurt contains active culture and is not pasteurized. Let the mixture stand a day or two in a warm place, lightly covered. When the cream is as sour as you want, refrigerate it.

SPAGHETTI: see PASTA

SPICES: see HERBS AND SPICES

SPINACH
- 1 pound of fresh spinach, cooked, will serve 2 people.
- 1½ pounds of spinach, cooked, drained, and chopped, will give you 1 cup.
- if fresh spinach begins to wilt, sauté it lightly with a very little bit of bacon fat and serve it hot. Or chill the spinach after you've sautéed it, add croutons, and serve as a salad.

SQUASH AND PUMPKINS
- see also *Zucchini.*

SQUASH
- soft-skinned squash, called summer squash (green zucchini, yellow crookneck, etc.), should have a shiny surface—a sign of freshness.
- choose squash, both summer and winter varieties, that are heavy for their size.
- acorn squash should have a dark-green rind—a sign of good quality.
- winter squash (acorn, butternut, Hubbard, etc.) are often hard to cut when raw. A small serrated meat saw does a better job than a knife and is safer because it's less likely to slip.
- winter varieties of squash are easily seeded and destringed at the same time if you use a serrated grapefruit spoon. An ice-cream scoop is also handy for removing the seeds quickly and neatly.
- use the flesh of any winter squash in place of pumpkin in a pie.
- a little grated raw winter squash or pumpkin is a fine extender for meat loaf or hamburger.
- you can pickle any type of winter squash or pumpkin just as you do watermelon rind. But in the case of squash and pumpkin, pare off the hard outer shell and pickle the flesh, in

chunks. Use the same spices and technique as for watermelon rind, and heat the pieces in the pickling liquid until they become translucent.

PUMPKINS

▪ peel and seed a pumpkin, cut it into chunks, then slice it thin, and dry it in a very low oven. When dried, the slices can be ground into flour in the blender. This is marvelous to use as part of the white or whole wheat flour in muffins, bread, etc.

▪ you can make pumpkin soup the same way you make potato soup. It cooks even more quickly. (Add a little milk at the end, but don't boil the soup.)

▪ why not cook and serve pumpkins as a vegetable? They're as good as squash and can be served in the same way.

STAINS

▪ salt combined with a little lemon juice or vinegar will usually remove burn stains from the outside of enamel-covered pots.

▪ stains can often be removed from a teapot spout if you pack the spout with salt, let stand overnight, and in the morning heat the teapot slightly and then pour boiling water through the spout. Or use a pipe cleaner, or two of them twisted together, to clean tannin stains and other deposits that accumulate in the spout of a teapot.

▪ yellow or gray stains in cups often are caused by the minerals in water, which, when combined with tea and coffee, leave deposits. You can get rid of the deposits by putting a teaspoon of baking soda in each cup, fill with very hot water, and let stand an hour or so. Wash well afterward.

▪ many mineral and tannin stains can be removed from the insides of cups by pouring in some salt, then rubbing well with your fingers moistened with water or vinegar.

STARCHES: see THICKENERS

STEAK: see MEATS

STEW
- see also *Meats.*
- if you want the gravy in a stew to have a lovely amber color, and the meat to taste twice as good, sprinkle a little sugar over the pieces of meat after the initial browning in the fat. (Use very little sugar.) Toss well over moderate heat for a few minutes until the sugar has caramelized.
- meat stew cooks even better in the oven (at about 325° F) than on top of the stove. The pot should have a heavy cover. Check now and then to see if a little liquid is needed.
- add a tablespoon of caraway seeds to the liquid of a meat stew, regardless of what kind of meat you use. Cook for at least 20 minutes after that.

STORAGE TIPS
- see also *Labels, Vegetables.*
- there's nothing like a glass jar with a tight-fitting lid for storage. It keeps the insides fresh and prevents contamination of other foods. Keep spare jars and lids of all sizes.
- it's wise to store the following foods in the freezer to keep them from deteriorating: all whole grain flours, shelled nuts, cans or bags of coffee, jars of instant coffee, brown rice, cornmeal. If there's no room in the freezer for them, at least refrigerate them. Many contain natural oils that become rancid at room temperature if they stand for long. Yeast keeps longer in your freezer, too.
- try to store refrigerated (and other) foods in jars instead of plastic bags. Plastic releases gases, and it's possible these may affect the foods stored in them.

■ anything stored in the refrigerator should be tightly covered not only to keep odors in, but also to keep moist foods from becoming dry. Frost-free refrigerators, especially, pull moisture out of the air and out of uncovered dishes.

■ if you have to store meat in the refrigerator a bit longer than you usually would, dust all the surfaces well with ground white or black pepper. Wipe it off with a damp cloth when you're ready to prepare the meat.

■ a sensible way to store granulated sugar is to pour it through a funnel into clean, dry, quart (or larger) bottles, such as pop bottles, with screw caps. When you need to measure out sugar or fill your sugar bowl, pour straight into the bowl or measuring cup. And *before* you pour, give the bottle a few hefty shakes to break up any small lumps. Sugar stored in a dry, narrow-necked bottle pours out like a dream, is easy to measure, and never cakes into a hard lump.

■ some peanut butter comes in large jars that are a perfect shape to use for storage. They're wider at the top than at the bottom. Stored foods slide out easily from jars of this shape.

■ quart milk containers are great for freezer storage. Wash and dry them thoroughly, and fill with either solids or liquids. Seal them well, label, and store. Once frozen, they can be stacked neatly in the freezer.

■ wash, rinse, and save a few of the waxed containers milk comes in. They're excellent for stacking cookies that you have to carry somewhere. They're also handy for pouring waste fats in. You'll find your own uses for them.

■ use the plastic tops of containers to set under jars and bottles kept in the refrigerator. They help keep the refrigerator shelves clean. Use for cupboard storage shelves, also. Set them under bottles of oil, syrup, or anything that tends to drip after you've used it.

■ if you nail the covers of screw-top jars to the undersides of cupboard shelves, you can fill the jars with herbs, spices, dried legumes, noodles, etc., and screw them into their tops. A handy, convenient place for storage.

■ pasta, well wrapped and stored in a cool, dry place, will keep for about 1 year (6 months for pasta containing eggs).

■ the extra-large jars of instant coffee make excellent storage jars for spaghetti and macaroni. They're narrow and high and the contents are immediately visible. Break the strands in half and stuff them in. One of these tall jars holds an 8-ounce package of spaghetti, keeping it dry and safe.

■ the trays inside your kitchen drawers will stay in place and not slide back every time the drawers are opened if you stuff something behind the trays. The cardboard cylinders inside the rolls of paper towels or toilet paper are very good for this.

■ slip the cardboard cylinder that's inside a roll of toilet paper over the spout of a delicate teapot when you're not using it. The cylinder will help keep the spout from getting chipped or broken.

■ S-hooks are handy items to hang things on in the kitchen. Slip them over a cupboard door or handle, or anywhere else they will fit.

STRAINERS

■ wash a strainer immediately after you use it so the holes won't get clogged. If you fail to do this and the holes *do* get clogged, soak the strainer to soften the food and then attack it with a soapy toothbrush.

■ cut off the panty and feet ends of panty hose. Save the nylon stocking parts; they make good strainers.

■ insert a wide-necked funnel into a piece of nylon stocking, draw the stocking tightly across the bottom opening of the funnel, and you have a fine strainer.

STRAWBERRIES: see BERRIES

STUFFING

- to make stuffing for a bird a couple of days ahead of time, mix all the wet ingredients and store them in a jar in the refrigerator. Mix the dry ingredients and set aside. When you're ready, combine them in a large bowl.

- it's actually best to prepare and refrigerate stuffing you make for chicken or turkey a day ahead. The flavors mingle and ripen, and you'll also save time and bustle on the day you roast the bird.

- to make a savory stuffing for chicken, use leftover bits of vegetables and meats. Mix with cubed bread, seasonings, and a little liquid.

- because stuffing expands during roasting, be sure you leave the skin around the stuffed cavity a little loose.

SUBSTITUTIONS

- one test of good cooks is what they do with food that has to be used up soon. Make substitutions. For example, in creamed spinach soup use string beans instead. Use zucchini. Use broccoli. Make unusual spaghetti sauces with whatever you have at hand. Practically anything goes, if you just use imagination and good sense.

SUGAR

- see also *Blender, Honey, Storage Tips.*
- to make a fine vanilla sugar, cut half of a long vanilla bean into tiny bits with a sharp knife. Put these in a mortar and pound with a pestle until well mashed. Measure ⅔ cup of granulated sugar and pour 2 tablespoons of it over the mashed vanilla bits. Pound vigorously. Continue adding 2 tablespoons of sugar at a time, pounding well after each addition, until all

the sugar is mixed in. The vanilla bits will look like black pepper. After you use some of the sugar (don't strain out the vanilla bits), replace it with the same amount of sugar, shake well, and store the jar again. The vanilla left in the jar will flavor sugar for well over a year.

■ grate lemon or orange peel, or a combination of both, and mix the pieces into a small jar of sugar. Cap this and use the flavored sugar, without straining, in cakes, cookies, icings, puddings, and tea.

■ use a clean, dry saltshaker when you need to shift sugar.

■ excess sweetness in a cooked dish can sometimes be disguised if you add a little mild vinegar while cooking.

■ before you add powdered sugar to a batter or icing, run the sugar in the blender to eliminate the lumps.

■ when a recipe calls for sifted confectioners' sugar, run the sugar in the blender for a few seconds instead of sifting.

■ 1 cup of brown sugar, well packed, weighs about 7 ½ ounces or 210 grams.

■ if you keep brown sugar well wrapped in the refrigerator, it rarely hardens or becomes lumpy.

■ if brown sugar *should* end up in one hard lump (because you didn't store it properly), you can always grate it, just as you do a piece of hard cheese. Or put it in the blender.

■ if you need brown sugar and don't have any, mix ½ cup of granulated sugar and 2 tablespoons of molasses with a whisk or wooden spoon. You'll get pretty much the equivalent of ½ cup of brown sugar.

SWEET POTATOES AND YAMS

■ 1 pound of sweet potatoes or yams will serve 3 people.

■ sweet potatoes don't keep as well as regular white potatoes, so don't buy them for long storage. And they must be kept dry. They deteriorate rapidly in a humid atmosphere.

■ sweet potatoes won't turn dark after they're peeled if you plunge them into salted water: 1 tablespoon of salt to 1 quart of water.

■ to make an interesting sweet potato flour, peel and slice raw sweet potatoes very thin. Dry them in the oven until they're as crisp as potato chips. Then grind into flour in the blender. Store in jars. Substitute for a portion of white or whole wheat flour for baking bread, muffins, etc.

SYRUP

■ syrup won't drip from a pitcher if you very lightly smear a bit of oil or butter across the inside of the pouring lip.

■ to make your own pancake and waffle syrups at a fraction of the cost of buying them, mix honey and molasses, a little vanilla extract and—if the mixture seems too thick—a tiny bit of water. Or thin it with a little frozen orange juice concentrate or any fruit juice for a fruit-flavored syrup. Heat gently, mix with a whisk, and pour into a bottle or small pitcher. (You can also add some broken nutmeats if you like.)

■ corn syrup and honey can be used in interchangeable amounts in baking.

■ the finest grade of maple syrup (which rarely reaches most markets) is very pale, almost waterlike, in color and has a mild maple flavor. This is Grade AA and is the product of the first sap flow in the spring. Later season runs, Grades A, B, and C, produce a progressively darker color and a more pronounced maple flavor. (Most "maple syrups" you buy in cans and bottles are a mixture of corn or cane and maple syrups. Almost all have artificial maple flavor and color added.)

TABLECLOTHS

■ you can make beautiful tablecloths from new sheets. A couple of times a year, when stores have white sales, you often can buy attractively patterned, flat twin-bed sheets at very low prices. They come in many colors, are drip-dry, and it doesn't take long to cut them to size. You can even make round tablecloths out of them. Use a round vinyl cover for a pattern and hem the tablecloths when you have a little time on your hands. (Use the round vinyl cover underneath the tablecloth as a table protector.)

■ an old tablecloth is great to cool freshly baked cookies on. It's clean and porous.

TEA

■ 1 tea bag usually contains 1 teaspoonful of tea leaves, enough for one or two 6-ounce cups of tea, depending on the strength preferred.

■ ¼ pound of tea makes about 60 cups.

■ unlike coffee, tea doesn't deteriorate much with time. When you open a package of loose tea or tea bags, transfer the contents to a tight-capped jar and store in a dark place.

■ if you like teas with unusual flavors and don't want to pay a fortune for them, make your own. Pour loose tea in a jar and add small amounts of flavors that appeal to you in any combination: minced vanilla bean, whole cloves, cardamom seeds, anise, allspice, nutmeg, ginger, some cinnamon stick, etc. A piece of dried orange or lemon rind is also nice. Keep in an airtight jar.

■ for iced tea that will never cloud, pour cold water over the tea leaves, cover, and refrigerate for a day or two. Strain as you pour it over ice cubes. Strength varies according to taste, but begin with 3 teaspoons of tea leaves to every ¾ cup of cold water. If you find this too strong when you pour it over the ice, add some ice water.

■ to keep your teapot sweet-smelling and free of tea stains, rub the inside of the pot with a paste of baking soda and a little water, then wash and rinse well. (To clean the spout of a teapot, see *Stains*.)

THICKENERS

■ 1 teaspoon of potato flour (also called potato starch) has the thickening power of 1 tablespoon of white flour.

■ rice flour and barley flour, which give a more delicate texture to a sauce than regular flour, are sometimes hard to find. You can make your own by putting ¼ cup of raw rice or barley in the blender at high speed until the flour is fine. You don't need much for most thickening purposes.

■ if you're using flour as a thickener in gravy, sauce, or soup, be sure you cook the dish—after the addition of the starch—for at least 2 full minutes, stirring occasionally. This breaks down the starch and eliminates any chalky taste.

■ other thickeners for casseroles, stews, or soups are noodles, macaroni, or spaghetti broken into bits.

■ cook any flour-thickened liquid that can't be simmered over direct heat in a double boiler over hot water. This is the secret for achieving a smooth, velvety sauce. Use a whisk for stirring and you'll avoid lumps.

■ if you want to thicken a pot of soup, scoop up 1 or 2

cupfuls with plenty of solids in it, and run in the blender. Then pour the mixture back into the soup pot, stir, heat, and serve. It's remarkable what this thickening technique does to a pot of soup—and without adding a single calorie.

TOMATOES
- 2 smallish tomatoes, coarsely chopped, equal 1 cup.
- try to buy tomatoes when they're in season. Hothouse tomatoes rarely have as good a flavor as vine-ripened ones.
- use plum tomatoes to make homemade tomato sauce or tomato paste. They have more flesh and less moisture.
- a cracked tomato won't keep; use it right away. Spoilage starts at the crack.
- if you have more tomatoes than you can use immediately, keep them in a moderately cool spot, but don't put them in the refrigerator. Refrigerating fresh tomatoes for more than an hour can kill the fresh-tomato flavor.
- the sharpest knives may have a tough time cutting through the skin of a tomato. To slice it neatly, without squashing or losing juice, make a small incision with the point of the knife at each spot where you want to slice.
- you can freeze tomatoes to use in the future for stews, soups, sauces, etc. Cut the tomatoes in quarters or eighths and set them on a cookie sheet in the freezer. When the pieces are frozen, put them in a plastic bag and store in the freezer. No need to peel them first; the skins peel off like a breeze when the pieces begin to thaw.

TOMATO PASTE
- a 6-ounce can of tomato paste equals ⅔ cup.

TOMATO SAUCE
- a 15-ounce can of tomato sauce equals about 2 cups.

TUNA

- use flaked tuna for a salad or sandwich filling: It's less expensive than chunk or solid packed tuna. You can, of course, flake the more expensive tuna. A 6½- or 7-ounce can, after flaking, will give you over 1 cup.
- canned tuna comes packed in oil, broth, or water. If you're on a weight-reducing diet, read the labels on tuna cans. You'll save calories.

TURKEY

- heavier turkeys generally cost less per pound than lighter, smaller ones, and there's a larger proportion of meat to bone on the bigger ones.
- for an amazingly good stuffing, use nothing but apples. Peel, core, and stuff the bird with them. After the turkey is cooked, remove the apple stuffing and mix with gravy.
- it takes 2 to 3 days, depending on size, for a frozen turkey to defrost in the refrigerator. (It's preferable to defrost a turkey in the refrigerator because it will lose less of its juices.)
- because turkey wing tips often burn when a turkey is being roasted, cut them off before you put the turkey in the oven and throw them into your stockpot. Or freeze them with other odds and ends you're saving for the stockpot.

TURNIPS

- 1 pound of yellow or white turnips, diced, will give you about 4 cups.
- to reduce the odor when you cook turnips, add a little sugar to the cooking water.
- mashed turnips are delicious, but if you find their consistency a trifle thin, mash in one boiled potato.

VANILLA

- for a pure vanilla flavor in your puddings, sauces, etc., split an inch of vanilla bean and cook it with the other ingredients. Remove it when the cooking is finished. For cakes and cookies, open an inch of bean and scrape the insides well into the batter.

- vanilla will give a lovely odor to your refrigerator. Put a drop or two on a piece of folded paper towel or a bit of cotton and set it inside.

VEGETABLES

- see also the names of individual vegetables.

- if you want to serve delicate vegetables braised or sautéed (zucchini, summer squash, tomatoes, etc.) in slices, cook them in your widest pan so they'll keep their shape.

- when you're selecting onions or potatoes or carrots to use whole, as in a stew, be sure to choose all the vegetables of each kind as close to the same size as possible so they'll cook uniformly.

- withered vegetables often can be brought back to life if you let them stand for an hour or so in cold salted water.

- dehydrate vegetable bits by placing them in a large strainer and set the strainer over a heat register or radiator. Bottle them when they're dry and papery.

- use the leg of a nylon stocking for dehydrating vegetables or mushrooms. Knot one end and pop in the pieces of vegetables. Then knot the other end and hang up until the pieces are thoroughly dry. (There's no better place to hang it than an attic, but the kitchen does fine if it's not too humid.) Then bottle the pieces and keep them beside the stove. They come in handy when you need to add a little flavor to a dish.

■ never throw out the liquid in which you cook vegetables (or the juices from canned vegetables, either). Store the liquid in a closed jar in the refrigerator or freezer. Use it to cook other vegetables in. Soon it will be so full-flavored that you can use it as the base of a soup.

■ use in place of the water generally called for in bread recipes, the water you've cooked vegetables in. It will add marvelous flavor to the bread and will also add to the bread's nutritive value.

■ peel vegetables over a sheet of newspaper. When you're finished, roll up the paper with its contents and chuck it in the garbage.

■ you can make dehydrated vegetable powders in the blender (onion, garlic, celery, carrots, green and red pepper, mushroom, etc.) to use in soups and gravies.

■ leftover cooked or canned vegetables (green or yellow string beans, pimientos, red or green peppers, black olives, etc.) can have their refrigerator storage life extended if you first pour enough plain cooking oil over them to cover.

■ any parts of vegetables that seem too tough or coarse to be served as a vegetable can be cooked, then puréed in the blender. They become a flavorful, nutritious base for a cream soup.

■ you don't really need a steamer to steam vegetables. Put ¼ inch of water into a heavy saucepan (1 inch of water if the pan is a thin one), bring to a boil, then put in the vegetables and cover the pan tightly. Peek in to see if the water has returned to a boil. When it does, lower the heat so that the water bubbles slowly. Cover again. Keep peeking. Don't over-cook vegetables.

VINEGAR

- add ¼ teaspoon of salt to your vinegar cruet and the vinegar will stay clear.

- to make herbed vinegar, heat the vinegar to quite hot, but not boiling, before you pour it over the herbs. This will speed up the flavoring process.

- why not make fruit-flavored wine vinegar? Add preserves or jams to a jar of red or white wine vinegar and let stand for a few days. Use in salad dressings or add a little cream to it to make a sauce for meat or chicken.

WAFFLES

■ dip bread slices in leftover waffle batter, sauté as you would French toast. Marvelous with cinnamon and sugar, jam, preserves, or syrup.

WALNUTS: see NUTS

WATER

■ a pot of water can be brought to a boil much faster if you cover it. But be careful—it can boil over.

WATERMELON: see MELONS

WAXED PAPER

■ if you're wrapping dough in waxed paper for temporary refrigerator storage, be sure to use *heavy* waxed paper—the kind that's waxed on both sides. Some bargain waxed paper is so flimsy that doughs stick to it and it's a major chore to remove.

WHIPPED CREAM: see CREAM

WINE

■ a tablespoon of sherry does wonders for scrambled eggs and omelets. Beat it into the eggs before you cook them.

■ a rather tough chicken can be very much tenderized if

you marinate it overnight in the refrigerator with seasoned white wine or dry vermouth.

■ use red wine for basting a beef roast after it's halfway roasted. Burgundy is first-rate for this.

■ substitute white or red wine for cream to pour over berries when serving them as a dessert.

■ it's a good idea, just before you serve a sauce or a soup made with wine, to add a tablespoon or so of the wine after the pot is taken off the heat.

■ pour a little port wine over baked apples just before you take them from the oven.

■ when you sauté any food, add a little wine to the pan to braise the contents. Be sure you lower the heat first and add the wine a little at a time, otherwise the wine and fat mixture will spatter.

■ if you're poaching fish for no more than 4 people, use white wine and seasonings instead of water. (Poaching for more than 4 will require at least 2 bottles.) And don't throw the poaching liquid out afterward—use it as the base of a fish sauce, or a fish or seafood chowder. You can freeze it.

■ substitute wine (white, red, or rosé) for the liquid called for in your meat loaf recipe.

YAMS: see SWEET POTATOES AND YAMS

YEAST AND YEAST DOUGH

■ you can bring any yeast quickly to a light foam by adding ¼ teaspoon of sugar to the water in which you dissolve the yeast. A pinch of ginger also speeds yeast action.

■ most yeast doughs refrigerate well for 2 or 3 days. You can make the dough one day and bake it a day or two later. Just be sure to let it come to room temperature again before you handle it. And it should be allowed to rise once, at least, before baking.

■ sweet raised yeast dough needs less kneading than regular bread dough.

■ yeast stored well wrapped in the freezer will stay in good condition for about 6 months.

■ too much yeast in yeast dough will make bread grow stale more quickly.

■ many bread recipes call for more yeast than is necessary. For every 3 cups of flour, 1 level teaspoon of yeast granules is enough. If you double the amount of flour, add only ½ teaspoon more of yeast.

■ don't let yeast dough stand too long during the final rising just before it goes into the oven, otherwise it is likely to fall during baking. The dough should rise until it's doubled in volume, no longer.

YOGURT

- see also *Sour Cream.*
- many of the flavored yogurts you buy in stores contain imitation flavoring and coloring. Why not buy plain yogurt and do the flavoring yourself? Add any fruits or berries you like, as well as honey, jam, syrups, etc. Yogurt is good mixed with salad vegetables, too.
- you can freeze yogurt and make a delightful dessert. First mix the yogurt with chopped fruit or nuts or both, then pour into a loaf pan and wrap well. Freeze. Serve it sliced with or without a sweet sauce.
- yogurt contains less fat and is more nutritious than sour cream. Substitute it for sour cream in baking as well as in custards, salad dressings, and sauces.

ZUCCHINI

- see also *Squash and Pumpkins.*
- 4 medium zucchini weigh about 1½ pounds and, unpared and thinly sliced, will give you about 5 cups.
- 1 pound of zucchini will serve 4 people generously.
- don't buy zucchini that are soft or wrinkled. They won't have a good texture or much taste.
- zucchini are done as soon as the skin gives easily when pressed. Don't overcook.
- cut well-scrubbed raw zucchini into almost paper-thin slices to use with other greens in a salad. The best zucchini for this are very young, slender ones.
- you can substitute zucchini in practically any recipe calling for cucumbers. It makes marvelous relish, too. Use any cucumber relish recipe.

ABOUT THE AUTHOR

In addition to being an accomplished cook and food authority descended from a family of chefs, Frieda Arkin is a lauded novelist and short story writer. A resident of Essex, Massachusetts, she was recently featured in *Yankee* magazine in their interview series, "Great New England Cooks." She writes a weekly newspaper column for the local *North Shore Sunday.*